Acc
Praying for Priest
for the Salvation oj

In this timely work, Kathleen Beckman presents the reader with practical ways to be prayerful supporters of those in Sacred Orders who, like Moses, are in need of the intercession of others to be able to successfully maneuver through the battlefield of the world and spread the message of salvation, available only through Jesus Christ, to a people hungering to hear it. While it is true that all the faithful are called to holiness, deacons, priests, and bishops must, in a particular way, practice virtue in order to fulfill the promises they make on their ordination day.

—**Archbishop J. Augustine Di Noia, O.P.**
Titular Archbishop of Oregon City

Praying for Priests: An Urgent Call for the Salvation of Souls is an eloquent reflection on the reality of the prayerful support needed by priests and bishops. I especially recommend the Scriptural Rosaries for priests, vocations, and reparation. They combine important contemporary needs with a very powerful and proven prayer to the Mother of God.

—**Most Reverend Kevin W. Vann**
Bishop of Orange, California

Kathleen Beckman's book is a masterful work of spiritual simplicity and richness. Drawing upon the Church's treasury of prayers expressive of our Apostolic Faith, she offers to priests and laity alike the graced opportunity to support, strengthen, and console every priest of the Lord Jesus in his priestly life of sacrificial service. I recommend this book to everyone who takes seriously the clarion call of the New Evangelization. To pray for another's spiritual and temporal well-being is an act of true mercy, and to pray for our priests sets the good example of a lived faith for others. I recommend making this book a part of your day, every day.

—**Most Reverend David D. Kagan**
Bishop of Bismarck, North Dakota

Praying for Priests reminds everyone that one of the most essential works of the laity to support clergy is to pray for priests. Prayer on behalf of priests was highlighted by the recent official publication of the Congregation for the Clergy, *Eucharistic Adoration for the Sanctification of Priests*. Kathleen wonderfully takes the efforts begun by that publication and her own life and work several steps further, explaining important efforts to make this message better known and more intelligible for contemporary women and the contemporary world. This is a book that will move you and make you redouble your efforts to pray for clergy!

—Msgr. Richard Soseman
Official of the Congregation for the Clergy and author of
Reflections from Rome: Practical Thoughts on Faith and Family

When attacks on the priesthood seem to be intensifying, Kathleen Beckman encourages and equips all the faithful to take up the power of prayer and spiritual fellowship, and in a special way calls upon women in the Church to embrace more deeply Jesus's invitation to become spiritual mothers for His priests. This book is of great value for this important and timely mission.

—Msgr. John R. Cihak, S.T.D.
Official at the Holy See and co-author
of *The Catholic Guide to Depression*

Praying for Priests is filled with insight, encouragement, and inspiration to lead both priests and laity to a more profound love of God's priceless gift of the priesthood.

—Fr. Peter John Cameron, O.P.
Editor of *Magnificat* and author of
Jesus, Present Before Me: Meditations for Eucharistic Adoration

Kathleen Beckman shows us a way to make the blessings of the priesthood outshine and overpower a myriad of new challenges confronting priests: an increasingly secularized culture, the new atheism, shadows cast by scandal, and pressures produced by the decline in vocations. As a priest,

I am both grateful and indebted to her for the rich graces that will come through this work of prayer.

—**Fr. Robert J. Spitzer, S.J., Ph.D.**
President of the Magis Center of Reason and Faith
and author of *New Proofs for the Existence of God:
Contributions of Contemporary Physics and Philosophy*

The Holy Spirit is really moving in the Church today, inspiring many women to become spiritual mothers for priests. Kathleen Beckman's new book gives a powerful boost to this movement as it offers practical advice and personal testimony that will help countless others to better understand and more fully embrace this beautiful calling.

—**Fr. Michael Gaitley, M.I.C.**
Author of '*You Did It to Me*': *A Practical Guide to
Mercy in Action* and *33 Days to Morning Glory*

In her work *Praying for Priests*, Kathleen Beckman manifests the deep love for priests that lies at the heart of her calling in providing this wonderful resource for those experiencing a similar call. This book's focus on praying for the *interior renewal of priests* points to the hidden fountain which is meant to strengthen the hearts of priests as they live their vocation in these challenging times. Kathleen's practical suggestions will invite many to join her in this vital mission.

—**Fr. Richard J. Gabuzda**
Executive Director, The Institute for Priestly Formation

Praying for Priests manifests Kathleen Beckman's many grace-filled experiences with priests and seminarians. The world is sorely in need of the Lord's gifts mediated through his chosen men. Through the lens of the teachings of the Church, Kathleen demonstrates the importance of sacramental priesthood and priestly ministry. I pray her work touches many hearts!

—**Fr. Abbot Eugene Hayes, O. Praem., J.C.D.**
St. Michael's Norbertine Abbey (Silverado, California)

Praying for Priests is a tangible expression of the powerful words of St. John Vianney: "The priest continues the work of redemption on earth.... The priesthood is the love of the Heart of Jesus." Kathleen Beckman's inspiring book is a compelling reminder to all Catholics of their sacred responsibility to pray unceasingly for our beloved priests.

—Mother Judith Zuniga, O.C.D.
Superior General, Carmelite Sisters
of the Most Sacred Heart of Los Angeles

Praying for Priests couldn't have arrived at a better time! At this moment in history, the Church and her priests are under attack and need the powerful protection of prayer more than ever. In my work with women, I have learned that part of our giftedness is a heart for others; I have seen firsthand the fruits that come when women exercise their gift of spiritual maternity through prayer. Thank you, Kathleen, for a thoughtful reflection that instructs, encourages, and inspires.

—Therese A. Polakovic
Foundress, Endow (Educating on
the Nature and Dignity of Women)

Kathleen Beckman provides Catholic women with the means to yoke themselves to the spiritual maternity of the Blessed Virgin Mary, be a conduit of grace in the lives of the men who are *in persona Christi*, and thereby, as Fr. John Hardon, S.J., put it, "carry on Mary's role as Mother of the Church in our time." Congratulations, Kathleen, for providing a work that strikes at the hearts of women to let loose a stream of spiritual maternity that flows into the hearts, souls, and ministries of our priests!

—Johnnette S. Benkovic Williams
Founder and President of Women of Grace® and
Host of *Women of Grace*, seen and heard on
EWTN Television and Radio

ᴥ

Praying for Priests
An Urgent Call for the Salvation of Souls

Praying for Priests

An Urgent Call for the Salvation of Souls

by Kathleen Beckman, L.H.S.

Foreword by Fr. Mitch Pacwa, S.J.

SOPHIA INSTITUTE PRESS
Manchester, New Hampshire

Biblical references in this book are taken from the Catholic Edition of the Revised Standard Version of the Bible, copyright 1965, 1966 by the Division of Christian Education of the National Council of the Churches of Christ in the United States of America. Used by permission. All rights reserved.

Nihil obstat: Pia de Solenni, *Censor Librorum*
Imprimatur: ✠ Most Reverend Kevin W. Vann, J.C.D., D.D.
Bishop of Orange in California, October 2, 2018

Sophia Institute Press
Box 5284, Manchester, NH 03108
1-800-888-9344
www.SophiaInstitute.com

Sophia Institute Press® is a registered trademark of Sophia Institute.

Library of Congress Cataloging-in-Publication Data
Beckman, Kathleen.
    Praying for priests : an urgent call for the salvation of souls / by Kathleen Beckman, L.H.S. ; foreword by Fr. Mitch Pacwa, S.J.
        pages cm
    ISBN 978-1-622827-169 (pbk. : alk. paper) 1. Catholic Church—Prayers and devotions I. Title.
    BX2149.2.B43 2014
    248.3'2—dc23

*To St. John Paul II and
the priests and seminarians
who enrich my life*

✣

*Mary, Mother of Priests,
Icon of Spiritual Motherhood, and
Star of the New Evangelization,
pray for us.*

_ﾟ_

Contents

Part 1: The Urgency and Vision

Part 2: Rosary Reflections and Prayers

꙳

Foreword

When I entered Quigley Preparatory Seminary in September of 1963, well more than five hundred young men of that incoming class began their training for the priesthood on two campuses, preparing for ordination in 1975. We were expected to study for three hours each day, plus attend daily Mass, pray a daily Rosary, confess weekly, and completely refrain from dating. Vatican II went into its second session that fall; the civil rights movement had been stirred by Dr. Martin Luther King's "I Have a Dream" speech at the Washington Mall, and the first Catholic president was in the White House.

The excitement of working toward the priesthood in a world full of such hope began to unravel with the assassinations of President John F. Kennedy, Martin Luther King Jr., and Senator Robert Kennedy. The Vietnam War, the antiwar protests, race riots, and the sexual and drug revolutions made everything even worse.

The Church was not immune to these cultural crises, either. Sociologically, Catholics became well educated and wealthy as a group; many of them looked beyond their Catholic and ethnic ghettoes so as to join the cultural mainstream. Some Catholic religious leaders interpreted the summons of Pope John XXIII to examine the "signs of the times" as permission to evaluate

Catholic doctrine and practice by the standards set by the culture: the primacy of personal freedom, the need for self-expression, and the dictates of psychological health — which were in fact in great flux as various schools of psychology vied with each other.

Many religious and clergy felt free to leave their state of life because personal freedom was more important than the commitments they had made through their vows. Some of them defined their role in terms of the service or work they did and even placed such a priority on their work that they proclaimed that their work *was* their prayer. As a result, some of them thought that traditional prayer was not necessary, others thought that "imposed" prayer such as the Breviary stifled freedom, and others considered the Rosary old-fashioned and anti-ecumenical. Large numbers of seminarians left their training (only thirty-eight members of my preparatory-school seminary class were ordained), and new vocations dried up, while various experiments with liturgy, retreats, and spiritualities came and went. In addition, the general participation of the laity waned significantly as fewer people felt a need to share in these experiments.

Of course, God never abandoned the Church, and His grace stirred deeply through a variety of renewal movements — Cursillo, Charismatic Renewal, Marriage Encounter, a Marian movement in the 1980s, renewed Eucharistic adoration, and many others — that led to a rediscovery of the Catholic Faith and new insights into the depths of the Church's spiritual treasures. The post-conciliar popes demonstrated that they loved Christ and His people more than they cared for mere theories and theological fads. They communicated an excitement for and deep insight into the Faith. Interestingly, from the first year of Pope John Paul II's papal ministry, the number of new seminarians steadily began to rise.

Foreword

This book draws on the energy of the lay movements that have revivified the Church from the 1960s until the present. It draws deeply from the wisdom and insights of the post-conciliar popes and sets forth a way of integrating them so as to help laity and clergy continue the forward-looking trends of authentic Catholic life and spirituality.

Enter the pages of this book and search out the guidance to help you take your place in the Church's pilgrimage into this new springtime of faith—a time of storms, as accompanies every spring, and a time of growth that often results from the storms.

— Fr. Mitch Pacwa, S.J.

✳

Introduction

Laypeople should not underestimate their important role in the
Church. Fifty years ago, at the Second Vatican Council, the
Council Fathers stated:

> The sacred pastors know very well how much the laity
> contribute to the welfare of the whole Church. They
> know that they themselves were not established by
> Christ to undertake alone the whole salvific mission of
> the Church to the world, but that it is their exalted of-
> fice to be shepherds of the faithful and to recognize the
> latter's contribution and charisms in such a way that all,
> in their measure, will with one mind cooperate in the
> common task.[1]

Two generations have passed since the close of the Council on
December 8, 1965. The Church has experienced ups and downs
during that time. Most practicing Catholics would not find it
difficult to remember positive experiences they and their families have had with priests, often connected with the celebration

---

[1] Vatican Council II, *Lumen Gentium* (Dogmatic Constitution
on the Church), no. 30.

of a sacrament, visits to the parish school, regular celebration of Sunday Mass, and so forth. Sadly, not everyone's experiences have been positive, and the actions of some priests have had and will continue to have negative consequences for the Church and her members.

What are we to do? In November 2012, the Congregation for the Clergy rolled out an initiative promoting the sanctification of priests. The Congregation is responsible for, among other things, the "sanctification and effective exercise of [priests'] pastoral ministry."[2] As such, it wishes to involve as many as possible in praying for bishops, priests, and deacons. Experience shows that everyone's involvement in this regard is needed. This initiative is in line with the Church's exhortation that the entire Christian community foster vocations to the priesthood: "This duty especially binds Christian families, educators, and, in a special way, priests, particularly pastors."[3]

Kathleen Beckman, a laywoman devoted to praying both for priests in very specific ways and for vocations to the priesthood, was enthusiastic when she read the first booklet of the Congregation for the Clergy promoting the sanctification of priests in 2007. The same Congregation presented the initiative anew and more substantially in 2012, strongly encouraging individuals and groups to pray for priests' holiness. Kathleen became convinced of the Lord's hand in this initiative. She approached others who expressed their desire to offer their talents in this regard. Kathleen summarized and logically laid out an action plan to help promote the initiative. This was communicated to the then prefect, His Eminence Mauro Cardinal Piacenza,

---

[2] John Paul II, Apostolic Constitution *Pastor Bonus*, art. 95 §3.
[3] *Code of Canon Law*, canon 233 §1.

who wrote back indicating his pleasure and support. This book is one of the fruits.

Because Kathleen firmly believes that holier priests will lead to a holier Church, her principal desire is to encourage readers to pray for priests, to offer up sufferings and sacrifices for them, and to pray that families might encourage certain of their members to consider seriously that God might be calling them to the priesthood.

One might argue that priests should be responsible to pray for themselves. Indeed, seminarians are to be taught the necessity of prayer, the importance of setting aside time each day for mental prayer and other forms of prayer, such as the Liturgy of the Hours and the Rosary. Developing good habits of prayer in the seminary helps one to continue these ways as a priest. To be sure, priests are expected to pray in the above-mentioned ways. The Church earnestly recommends that priests celebrate the Holy Sacrifice of the Mass each day,[4] and we as priests are expected to be faithful to this expectation.

Yet the demands on priests can weigh heavily. Priests rely on the prayers of others. When others pray and offer up some of their sufferings for the Church, for priests, and for vocations to the priesthood, so much good is done. The Lord honors this. It is pleasing to Him. And His Mother, our Mother, indeed wishes to bring to the feet of her Son the intentions we present to her. Kathleen Beckman assists us in this regard by devoting all twenty mysteries of the Rosary to the sanctification of priests.

In addition, five Mysteries of Light are dedicated to praying for vocations to the priesthood. While most parishes in North America are at least able to "get by" with the priests they have,

---

[4] *Code of Canon Law*, canon 904.

there are other parts of the world where the people rejoice if a priest is able to get to their church once a year. So we should not limit our prayers for vocations only to our backyard but rather extend them to the universal Church. As the author mentions, those who perceive priests in a negative light will usually not encourage their sons to consider priesthood. With the help of your prayers, let us hope these perceptions will slowly become more positive and people will better understand the lofty vocation of the priest.

While this inspired book focuses primarily on the sanctification of priests, the author is not unaware that obstacles can prevent people from fully embracing this important initiative. There are those who suffer and are in need of our prayers. Some people have had a bad experience with a priest and remain unsettled. For others, news of the sexual abuse scandal has resulted in their leaving the Church. And with advances in technology, news of a priest who stumbles on the other side of the world is made public worldwide, giving some the impression that no priest can be trusted. Nor can the victims of sexual abuse be overlooked or forgotten; rather, they should be assisted in receiving the healing power of Jesus Christ. Of course, we are all in need of healing, but sometimes there are obstacles in the way. Forgiving others is not always easy. Realizing this, Kathleen Beckman devotes five Sorrowful Mysteries of the Rosary, along with reflections and petitions, to the healing of past and present hurts.

I can attest that the author practices what she preaches. She prays a daily Holy Hour in front of the Blessed Sacrament. Her experiences as a wife and mother have taught her much. Many people have opened up to her with their struggles and difficulties. She generously listens to them and prays for them. She is aware of difficulties facing priests and Catholics in general. Her involvement in healing and deliverance ministry has exposed her to the evil present in the world. All these things she takes to prayer regularly. This is how she was able to formulate the petitions and the particular intentions connected with each mystery of the Rosary.

I trust that you will find this book helpful, and I encourage you to be steadfast in your prayer. If this practice has slipped away, please do your best to regain it. If you have never really prayed, let the recitation of the mysteries of the holy Rosary be a healthy starting point. You will find these mysteries more enriching as you progress in your spiritual journey.

Finally, thank you for your interest in priestly holiness and for your desire to contribute to this mission.

—Msgr. Stephen Doktorczyk, J.C.D, M.B.A.,
Vicar General and Moderator of the Curia
Diocese of Orange, California

Part 1

ﺟ

The Urgency and Vision

1

༄

Urgency: Why We *Must* Pray for Priests

*When people want to destroy religion they begin by attacking
the priest; for when there is no priest, there is no sacrifice:
and when there is no sacrifice, there is no religion.*[5]
—St. John Vianney

Nearly every morning for the past twenty-five years, I have made
my way to the local church for Mass. There, together with an
average of three hundred parishioners, I'm absorbed in the beauty
of the liturgy, deeply grateful to receive the gift of God. Every
day, my parish priest is at the altar to offer sacrifice to the Eternal
Father on my behalf and on behalf of the entire Church. He is
there in the person of Jesus, the Eternal High Priest. At times
during the liturgy, I don't see the priest as anyone other than the
Lord's "other self"—I'm mindful of Jesus at the altar in his priest.

To say that the Church's liturgy enriches my daily life is an un-
derstatement. I know I am a sinner. Yet, through the sacramental

[5] Quoted in Abbé Alfred Monnin, *Life of the Curé d'Ars* (Balti-
more: Kelly and Piet, 1865), 281.

3

fountains of the Church, made possible by the ministerial priesthood, I'm a better wife, mother, daughter, sister, and worker in
God's vineyard. Having traveled to many countries over the past
twenty years in service of the Church, speaking and praying with
clergy, nuns, men, women, and families, my love for God and
His Church has only deepened.

I am writing the second edition of this book at the time when
we are experiencing anew the revelation of terrible clergy crimes,
the violation of a sacred trust from some whom we considered
shepherds and fathers. The weight of sorrow for the abuse victims
is unspeakable, as is the pain of betrayal by clergy.

Signs of problematic infidelities and illicit compromises in
key areas of the Church have been evident for years. The problem with small infidelities or compromises is that they lead to
bigger ones. Somehow human innovation eclipses the divine.
We've witnessed liturgies in which illicit insertions or omissions
are made. We know that the preacher is trying too hard to please
everyone when he waters down the hard truths of Jesus Christ.
Sexual immorality, including criminal sexual abuse, is a cancer
in and outside of the Church, but there are absolutely no excuses
for clergy to fall so far from God and grace, abandoning their
post and flock. Even a handful of clergy who have shamelessly
sinned and cooperated with evil is too many.

As for the laity, I'm not sure we have been as diligent and
generous in spiritually protecting and strengthening our priests
as is necessary to build up the Church. Now God has permitted
the light of truth to illumine the deeds of darkness perpetrated
by His own beloved priests. Thanks be to God! Let justice be
done and healing begin.

While it is difficult to perceive how the Church will recover
from the present crisis, she will most definitely recover. We hold

fast to God's Word: "And I tell you, you are Peter, and on this rock I will build my church, and the gates of hell will not prevail against it" (see Matt. 16:18). Our Father has a perfect plan. It will not be frustrated by sinners or the devil. God is greater than the Church's present mess.

How should we respond to the scandal caused by some priests? "The evidence of infidelity in priests should arouse in the hearts of Christ's faithful the wish to expiate," Fr. John Hardon, S.J., tells us. We can offer to repair the insult and injury done to the Lord and to souls by our steadfast faith, our prayer, our sacrifice, and the offering up of our suffering.

This defining moment in the Church begs for reforms of a temporal order, but these will be only as strong as the spiritual response of prayer, penance, and reparation that must undergird them. Atonement for the sins in the Church over too many decades will be required. Many people will leave the Church over this crisis, and we who remain will suffer ridicule and persecution for our fidelity. Like the first responders to any disaster, we can enter into this situation to be rebuilders of the breach. Love for God and the Church will help us to resist the temptation to hurl stones at clerics, the majority of whom are authentic good shepherds. Scripture proposes a better response: to share in the suffering of God's sinful people, and commit to *more* prayer, fasting, and almsgiving to atone for collective sins.

Whether you're reading this book during this crisis, or many years afterward, the urgency and vision are perennial. Christ looks to you to beautify His mystical Bride. As disciples, we know that praying for the holiness of priests is a sacred duty for the salvation of all souls.

We often implore prayers from priests, who are considered to be prayer experts. Their ministry accompanies us in the most defining moments of our lives. Recall the solemn beauty of infant Baptisms; the awe of First Holy Communions; the joy of Confirmations; the hopeful promise of sacramental weddings; the healing balm of sacramental Confession and Anointing of the Sick; the consoling rite of Christian burial, which lifts our tear-filled eyes toward heaven. In the priest's eyes we still dare to look for a glimpse of the Good Shepherd's loving, kind heart. The Lord instituted the sacrament of Holy Orders for love of you and me.

A Spiritual Battle Begs a Spiritual Response

Scripture reminds us, "The reason the Son of God appeared was to destroy the works of the devil" (1 John 3:8). Christ chose the Twelve to do the same. From start to finish, the life of Christ on earth reveals how the devil pursued Him—from Herod to Judas. The ancient serpent is unrelenting in his temptation of priests to mock Christ, to cease the perpetual sacrifice, and to render the Church impotent. Satan is a dealer of doubt, a sower of dissent, a divider, and a deceiver. Sexual sin and moral disorder are definitely the devil's playground. Priests have dire need of strong spiritual armor reinforced by the prayers and fasting of God's people. That is why informed Catholics are not surprised to be told, "You must always carry a special place in your prayers and in your heart for the sanctification of the priesthood and the sacredness of the Mass."[6]

There is an intimate unity between priests and the Eucharist. Every prayer that we offer for the holiness of priests helps to protect them *and the Eucharist* from demonic profanation. As part of an exorcist priest's team, I have witnessed that during the

---

[6] Fr. Gerald M. C. Fitzgerald, retreat at Parish Visitors of Mary Immaculate, June 28, 1942, quoted by Fr. John Hardon, S.J.

exorcism a demon is forced to attest to his hatred toward priests because of the Eucharist.

"The devil knows that every Mass gives immeasurable glory to the Divine Majesty, which he hates. So he does everything in his power to seduce priests in his camp so they will not offer Mass, or offer it less often, or less devoutly; anything to prevent God from being given the glory and souls from receiving the graces that flow from the Holy Sacrifice of the Mass," wrote Fr. Hardon.[7]

One example of a diabolical attack against a priest and the Eucharist is the case of French priest Fr. Jacques Hamel of recent history, who was murdered at the altar in the middle of a Mass. Eyewitness Sr. Danielle confirmed that, before dying, Fr. Hamel called out twice, "Be gone, Satan!" She added that "this does not mean that [the assailant] Adel Kermiche was possessed, but that Satan was at work in a powerful way. Father Jacques wanted to exorcise this evil. Those were his last words. Satan does not like the Eucharist."[8] The cause for the beatification of Fr. Jacques Hamel has begun. While some priests are instruments of destruction, other priests, in growing numbers, are heroically lifting up the Church by laying down their lives for the Faith.

Fr. Hardon addressed spiritual warfare:

Having taught priests over 30 years, having lived with priests, and having labored for them, loving them and suffering with them—no words I can use would be too

---

[7] Fr. John Hardon, S.J., *A Prophet for the Priesthood* (Kensington, MD, Inter Mirifica, 1998), 118.

[8] Quoted in Elizabeth Scalia, "Eyewitness Report: Father Jacques Hamel's Last Moments," Aleteia, October 4, 2016, https://aleteia.org/2016/10/04/witnesses-to-martyrdom-father-hamels-last-moments/.

strong to state that the Catholic priesthood needs prayer and sacrifice as never before since Calvary. One saint after another has declared that the devil's principal target on earth is the Catholic priest. Priests need, Lord how they need, special graces from God. We ask, why pray, then, for priests? We should pray for priests and bishops because this has been the practice of the Church since apostolic times. It's a matter of revealed truth. It is a divine mandate.[9]

The imagery of spiritual warfare is intentional because the Church Militant is in a battle against the world, the flesh, and the devil, as St. Paul taught (Eph. 6:12). Serving in the Church's ministry of deliverance and exorcism, I witness the intensity of the battle between good and evil. During the rite of exorcism we see the blatant aversion that demons have to the priest (his stole elicits diabolical screams), the Eucharist (demons cry out, "It burns me!"), and sacramentals such as the Rosary and holy water (which elicits shrieking). The devil seeks to tear priests away from Christ and stifle vocations.

For spiritual battles, God chose the Virgin Mary to crush the head of the serpent. She is the Queen Mother, fierce in battle, building an army for the King. We can bring priests to the Immaculate Heart for healing and strengthening. We implore the Virgin Mary to help us see priests with her eyes: "For her, a priest is always a priest, a living image of her Son, and if that image is disfigured by sin, she only has a more ardent desire to give him

---

[9] Fr. John Hardon, S.J., "The Value of Prayer and Sacrifice for Priests," Fr. John A. Hardon, S.J., Archives, The Real Presence Association, http://www.therealpresence.org/archives/Prayer/Prayer_014.htm.

back that resemblance to Christ, for she sees him as God sees him."[10]

The Ars Model: Priests, Warfare, Victory

Of St. John Vianney, the humble parish priest of the small town of Ars, France, during the 1800s, Pope John Paul II wrote:

> His example cannot be forgotten! More than ever we need his witness, his intercession, in order to face the situations of our times, when, in spite of a certain number of hopeful signs, evangelization is being contradicted by a growing secularization, when spiritual discipline is being neglected, when many are losing sight of the Kingdom of God, when often even in the pastoral ministry, there is a too exclusive concern for the social aspect, for temporal aims. In the last century, the Curé of Ars had to face difficulties which were perhaps of a different kind but which were no less serious.[11]

St. John Vianney preached on the unrelenting diabolical and human attacks against priests, sacrifice, and religion.

"In 1972, Pope Paul VI told nations reeling from hunger, violence, indolence, and nuclear threats that evil is not an absence of good: it is a 'living, spiritual being' who is perverted and perverts: What are the greatest needs of the Church today? Do not let our answer surprise you as being over-simple or even superstitious and unreal: one of the greatest needs is defense from that evil which is called the devil," reports Fr. George Rutler.

---

[10] Father Marie Dominique Philippe, O.P., quoted in *Magnificat Year for Priests Companion* (New York: Magnificat, 2009), 51.

[11] Fr. Fredrick L. Miller, *The Grace of Ars* (San Francisco: Ignatius, 2010), 141.

"And, Pope Paul VI publicly lamented that the smoke of Satan had even entered the Church. The warning redresses what has already become the quandary of Vianney's progressive culture."[12] It's remarkable that God's remedy for the quandary of France's progressive culture was a humble, courageous priest who is now the patron of all priests.

God permitted St. John Vianney, like Job, to be vexed, even tormented, by the devil, who tried to ruin him and his flock. "In the extraordinary events in Ars, which began in 1824 and lasted until a year before the saint's death, the terror and wonder of the confrontation between good and evil were palpable," wrote Fr. Rutler.[13] Today the battle between light and darkness is raging far beyond the town of Ars, France.

An incident from the life of St. John Vianney illustrates how clergy are God's essential soldiers. It was necessary for the saint to perform an exorcism when a woman hurled herself at him, shouting in a diabolical voice, "If there were three like you on earth, my kingdom would be destroyed. You have taken more than eighty thousand souls from me."[14] Let us beg God for more priests like St. John Vianney.

"The evil one terrorizes no one as much as he is terrified by Christ the Victor; a losing foe can still win incidental battles before the war's end, but the outcome for the world is certain even when individual fates are not."[15] We proclaim Christ's victory

---

[12] George William Rutler, *The Curé D'Ars Today*, repr. ed. (San Francisco: Ignatius Press, 2009), 161.

[13] Ibid., 162.

[14] George William Rutler, *The Cure D'Ars Today* (San Francisco: Ignatius Press, 1988), 174-175.

[15] Ibid., 171.

with every sacrifice on behalf of priests because prayer strengthens the watchmen.

Urgency for the Salvation of Souls

Each of us has a task to perform in the Church. According to our state of life, we have a responsibility to pray for many things, as Jesus taught. But priests have an exalted role in the Body of Christ because they alone can make Jesus present on the altar and can absolve us of our sins. Yet they remain human and in need of much grace. They have a responsibility to pray, and if they do not pray, they will fall into temptation. They have a special claim on our prayer support because of what their ministry means to us.

Father Raniero Cantalamessa, O.F.M. Cap., notes that the Holy Spirit is calling the laity to a new vocation to aid priests:

> The Lord today is calling the faithful in ever-growing numbers to pray, to offer sacrifices, in order to have holy priests. A concern, a passion, for holy priests has spread as a sign of the times throughout today's Church. The royal and universal priesthood of believers has found a new way of expressing itself: contributing to the sanctification of ministerial priesthood. Such vocations are extending out more and more beyond the walls of the cloistered monasteries, where they have been hidden, and are reaching the faithful.
>
> This vocation is becoming widespread, a call that God addresses to many. Through prayer, people are supporting the proclamation of the word and increasing its effectiveness and its fruitfulness. I share with you my time, my study, and the understanding that I acquired from the treasure

house of the Church, but others, who are unknown, have contributed the most precious thing: prayer and suffering.[16]

A priest once taught how our prayers intertwine with priests' ministry:

> Since Christ, who is Eternal Wisdom and Love, has deliberately chosen to use men for such a vital role, anytime anyone strengthens a priest or all priests, he or she strengthens the very hand of Christ, the heart of Christ, the lips of Christ, the eyes of Christ. If your prayer is universal, he is a priest strengthened by your prayers. You have helped Christ on that sick call if you are praying for priests and praying according to their needs in the Heart of Christ. You have helped today, the poor shivering ill-clad priest in Siberia, you have helped the faithful in their hideouts in China.[17]

More than two thousand years ago, the evangelist Luke recorded the Eternal High Priest: "The harvest is plentiful, but the laborers are few; pray therefore the Lord of the harvest to send out laborers into his harvest" (10:2). Christ mandates us to intercede for vocations because they are essential for human formation, the work of salvation.

Ministerial priests and laity are distinctively tasked with building up the kingdom of God. Priests are ontologically configured to Christ, the Head; the lay faithful make up Christ's Body. This

---

[16] Raniero Cantalamessa, O.F.M. Cap., *Sober Intoxication of the Spirit, Part Two: Born Again of Water and the Spirit* (Cincinnati: Franciscan Media), chap. 3, Kindle ed.

[17] Fr. John Hardon, S.J., quoting Fr. Gerald M.C. Fitzgerald, *A Prophet for the Priesthood* (Kensington, MD: Inter Mirifica, 1998), 117.

implies mutual honor, for the Body of Christ. "If one member suffers, all suffer together; if one member is honored, all rejoice together" (1 Cor. 12:26). It would be unfitting for us to draw from the goods of ministerial priesthood without reciprocal spiritual return to them.

"Behold, I send you out as lambs in the midst of wolves," Christ said (Luke 10:3). Today believers experience the weight of witnessing to Christ as "lambs in the midst of wolves," for the enemies of Christ are many, cunning, and unrelenting. Foremost, priests experience the weight of lifting the Cross of Jesus in a faithless world, where they are a neon sign of contradiction. The Church is the target of calculated persecution and evil.

"For Such a Time as This"

Therefore, "for such a time as this" (Esther 4:14), the Church beseeches the laity to embrace our mission as intercessors. "But our prayer to God does not consist of words alone; the words must lead to actions so that from our praying heart a spark of our joy in God and in the Gospel may arise, enkindling in the hearts of others a readiness to say yes," wrote Pope Benedict XVI.[18] The complete passage from the book of Esther reads, "For if you keep silence at such a time as this, relief and deliverance will rise for the Jews from another quarter, but you and your father's house will perish. And who knows whether you have not come to the kingdom for such a time as this?" Esther had a difficult, vital mission that she courageously completed, saving her people from extermination by the Persian king Ahasuerus.

---

[18] Quoted in Congregation for the Clergy, *Eucharistic Adoration for the Sanctification of Priests and Spiritual Maternity* (Fort Collins, CO: Books for Catholics, 2012), 11.

We can intuit the same question aimed at us: "Who knows whether you have not come to the kingdom for such a time as this?" Present challenges call forth a new movement of intercessory prayer, an army of prayer groups and individuals who will say yes to helping the priests to push back the tsunami of sin and evil. At stake is the salvation of souls and the evangelization of future generations. In the Old Testament, Esther put her life on the line to fulfill her mission, as did the holy ones who lived before us. This is the hour for which we are chosen. The battle is the Lord's (see 2 Chron. 20:15), but we're His essential soldiers.

Holy Orders: Necessity, Beauty, Challenge

Christ calls forth a communion of people, relationships of love in which people contribute with complementary gifts to build up the human family. Jesus sets the example on several occasions in the Gospels when He humbly accepts the help of others and commissions people to assist in His work. The Lord never intended for priests or laity to walk alone or apart. Like the human body, Christ's Mystical Body is deliberately integrated: "For just as the body is one and has many members, and all the members of the body, though many, are one body, so it is with Christ" (1 Cor. 12:12).

The *Catechism of the Catholic Church* describes Holy Orders as "the sacrament through which which the mission entrusted by Christ to His apostles continues to be exercised in the Church until the end of time: thus it is the sacrament of apostolic ministry" (no. 1536). In presenting himself for Holy Orders, a man steps out in faith, into a mystery far greater than himself. It takes fortitude for a man to enter the seminary and be ordained in this age. What makes possible the total gift of self to God? Only love. A person in love with God "bears all things, believes all things, hopes all things, endures all things" (1 Cor. 13:7).

This is the science of love personified in Jesus. One who allows himself to be captured by divine love is an instrument in God's hand. This means the priest must possess a kind of availability of spirit, as Pope Benedict XVI wrote:

> Day after day it is necessary to learn that I do not possess my life for myself. Day by day I must learn to abandon myself; to keep myself available for whatever he, the Lord, needs of me at a given moment, even if other things seem more appealing and more important to me: this means giving life, not taking it.[19]

The life that priests give to us is Christ-life: His body and blood for food, His mercy for forgiveness, His word that protects, His love that heals, His truth that sets us free.

Commenting on St. John Vianney's statement, "The priest is the love of the Heart of Jesus," Pope Benedict XVI writes. "The expression of Saint John Vianney also makes us think of Christ's pierced Heart and the crown of thorns which surrounds it. I also think, therefore, of the countless situations of suffering endured by many priests, either because they themselves share in the manifold human experience of pain or because they encounter misunderstanding from the very persons to whom they minister."[20] Priests' hearts will be pierced as was the Lord's.

To that point, among the Lord's messages to an anonymous Benedictine monk in his book *In Sinu Jesu* is this: "It is in my suffering priests that I live my victimhood and bring many souls to

---

[19] Pope Benedict XVI, Homily at Ordination Mass for 15 deacons of the Diocese of Rome, Rome, May 7, 2006.
[20] Pope Benedict XVI, Inaugural Letter for the Year for Priests, 2009.

salvation who, were it not for My Passion continued in my priests, would be lost to my love for them. I will save souls through the sufferings of My victim priests. They are lambs for the slaughter, but I am their life, and their sufferings and death are precious in my sight."[21] Priests are foremost intercessors for us.

Priests Affect Our Growth in Holiness

St. Peter taught, "As obedient children, do not be conformed to the passions of your former ignorance, but as he who called you is holy, be holy yourselves in all your conduct; since it is written, 'You shall be holy, for I am holy'" (1 Pet. 1:14-16). Intercession for priests has everything to do with the universal call to holiness.

"As the shepherd, so the sheep; as the priest, so the people. Priest-victim leadership begets a holy Church. Every worldly priest hinders the growth of the Church; every saintly priest promotes it. If only all priests realized how their holiness makes the Church holy and how the Church begins to decline when the level of holiness among priests falls below that of the people!"[22]

It is true also that "holy Christians guarantee holy priests."[23] If we desire to be inspired by holy priests, we also should mirror holiness for them. Writing to priests about their effect on others, Venerable Archbishop Fulton J. Sheen penned, "Every slightest failing on our part brings the community under the judgment of God. Every least increase of priestly virtue brings it blessing."[24] Mutual support is vital. Have we grown comfortable

---

[21] *In Sinu Jesu* (Kettering, OH: Angelico Press, 2016), 262.
[22] Fulton Sheen, *The Priest Is Not His Own* (San Francisco: Ignatius Press, 2005), 76-77.
[23] Ibid., p. 79.
[24] Ibid., p. 83.

with receiving the goods of the priesthood without reciprocal charity and service?

If the priest is to remain completely available to God and His people, willing to embrace suffering, *he needs perennial renewal.* St. Gregory of Nazianzus wrote of this:

> We must begin by purifying ourselves before others; we must be instructed to be able to instruct, become light to illuminate, draw close to God to bring him close to others, be sanctified to sanctify, lead by the hand and counsel prudently. I know whose ministers we are, where we find ourselves and to where we strive. I know God's greatness and man's weakness, but also his potential. Who then is the priest? He is the defender of truth, who stands with angels, gives glory with archangels, causes sacrifices to rise to the altar on high, shares Christ's priesthood, refashions creation, restores it in God's image, recreates it for the world on high and, even greater, is divinized and divinizes.[25]

People ask me, "What about our families?" I reply, "Praying for priests is a service to the family." Vital to each family member are the sacramental goods of the Church. We are serving the spiritual life of the family when we pray for priests and vocations. God is never outdone in generosity. For many years, it has been my experience that when I pray first for God's intentions in His priests, the Lord abundantly blesses my family.

Vesting Priests in Spiritual Garments: Prayer Power

The Apostle John wrote, "And this is the confidence which we have in Him, that if we ask anything according to his will, he

---

[25] Quoted in *Catechism of the Catholic Church* (CCC), no. 1589.

hears us. And if we know that he hears us in whatever we ask, we know that we have obtained the requests made of him" (1 John 5:14-15). The power of prayer cannot be underestimated. Its primacy is expressed by St. John Vianney:

> Prayer is the source of all graces, the mother of all virtues, the efficacious and universal way by which God wills that we should come to him. He says to us: "Ask, and you shall receive." None but God could make such promises and keep them. He says to us, "If you ask the Father anything in my name, he will give it to you." ... Ought not this promise to fill us with confidence, and to make us pray fervently all the days of our poor life? Within the reach of the ignorant, enjoined to the simple and to the enlightened, prayer is the virtue of all mankind; it is the science of all the faithful! Everyone on earth who has a heart, everyone who has the use of reason ought to love and pray to God.[26]

Such an edifying exhortation! St. Matthew reminds us, "And He said to them, "It is written, 'My house shall be called a house of prayer'; but you make it a den of robbers" (Matt. 21:13). Let us preserve the Church as a "house of prayer" and be people of deep communion with God. Only then will we be lights in the darkness (see Matt. 5:14), salt of the earth (Matt. 5:13), warriors for Christ.

The Role of the Laity

Pope John Paul II articulates the role of the lay faithful in his apostolic exhortation *Christifideles Laici*:

> *You go too.* The call is a concern not only of Pastors, clergy, and men and women religious. The call is addressed to

[26] Quoted in Magnificat Year for Priests Companion (2009), 28.

everyone: lay people as well are personally called by the Lord, from whom they receive a mission on behalf of the Church and the world. In preaching to the people Saint Gregory the Great recalls this fact and comments on the parable of the laborers in the vineyard: "Keep watch over your manner of life, dear people, and make sure that you are indeed the Lord's laborers. Each person should take into account what he does and consider if he is laboring in the vineyard of the Lord."[27]

Pope Paul VI exhorts the laity on obligations to their priests:

The Christian faithful, for their part, should realize their obligations to their priests ... sharing their cares, they should help their priests by prayer and work insofar as possible so that their priests might more readily overcome difficulties and be able to fulfill their duties more fruitfully.[28]

Fr. Cantalamessa suggests that the contribution of the laity for the ministerial priesthood is vital for their ministry:

The royal and universal priesthood of believers has found a new way of expressing itself: contributing to the

---

[27] St. John Paul II, *Christifideles Laici*, December 30, 1988, no. 2, http://w2.vatican.va/content/john-paul-ii/en/apost_exhortations/documents/hf_jp-ii_exh_30121988_christifideles-laici.html. An apostolic exhortation is a formal type of communication from the Holy Father that can be addressed to one or more groups and often reinforces a Church teaching. In *Christifideles Laici*, Pope John Paul II lays out a mission for how the laity can live out their Baptism and the values of the Gospel in communion with the Church in today's world.

[28] Pope Paul VI, *Presbyterorum Ordinis*, December 7, 1965, no. 9.

sanctification of ministerial priesthood. Such vocations are extending out more and more beyond the walls of the cloistered monasteries, where they have been hidden, and are reaching the faithful. This vocation is becoming widespread, a call that God addresses to many. Through prayer, people are supporting the proclamation of the word and increasing its effectiveness and its fruitfulness. I share with you my time, my study, and the understanding that I acquired from the treasure house of the Church, but others, who are unknown, have contributed the most precious thing: prayer and suffering. [29]

The Church's Vision

The Congregation for the Clergy's document *Eucharistic Adoration for the Sanctification of Priests and Spiritual Maternity* states, "Throughout its over two thousand year history, the Catholic Church, established by Our Lord as the instrument of salvation for mankind, has suffered countless crises precipitated by the weakness of its members. Priests, in particular, face many challenges, striving to do the will of God at every moment of their lives, yet confronted with the countless temptations of modern life. These temptations are best overcome with prayer and penance, their own, and the prayers of others on their behalf. Indeed, spiritual writers through history have explained the necessity of prayer for the fruitful ministry of priests."[30]

We should explain that the Congregation's vision of spiritual maternity of priests, consists of a woman's participation in the

---

[29] Cantalamessa, *Sober Intoxication*, 60-61.
[30] *Eucharistic Adoration for the Sanctification of Priests and Spiritual Maternity*, 8.

universal motherhood of Mary, who is the Mother of the Eternal High Priest and, therefore, the mother of all priests. They propose that behind all priests there is a spiritual mother who asked God for their vocation; or atones for their failings, and contributes to their growth in virtue and sanctity by the intentional offering of her daily activities and suffering. This vital role for women will be further developed in the chapter on the Church's history of spiritual motherhood.

A profound Marian transformation occurs in a woman's soul to enable her to imitate Mary's spiritual maternity for priests. It's frequently a hidden vocation of self-sacrificing spiritual service. The same could be said of spiritual fatherhood for clergy in imitation of St. Joseph. The Lord led me into deeper understanding of this call for the broader Church while on pilgrimage to the Holy Land. On a private retreat with a handful of priest friends in Jerusalem in 2013, during nocturnal prayer at the Church of the Holy Sepulchre, I reflected on the Congregation for the Clergy's initiative for priests. The inspiration arose to seek permission to spread their vision internationally. Seeing the need, the priests agreed. Upon returning home, we wrote our proposal and sent it to Rome.

Two months later, on the Feast of the Visitation (May 31) a letter from the papal nuncio arrived. Reading the positive response, I knew the Lord honored what was placed on our hearts during that cold rainy night at Calvary. Fortified by the encouragement given us by the former prefect of the Congregation for the Clergy, His Eminence Mauro Cardinal Piacenza, an apostolate was formed with a team of clergy and laity. A website and media campaign were launched, and this book was written. Since the Foundation of Prayer for Priests began in 2013, thousands of priests, religious sisters, consecrated communities, men, women, and families spanning fifteen countries have joined this work—still in its infancy.

While the original document does not include spiritual fatherhood of priests, we were told by the prefect's secretary in a meeting in Rome that the Congregation desired us to engage spiritual fathers for priests and seminarians. In another meeting in Rome, with Archbishop Patrón Wong, a secretary in the Congregation for the Clergy, we were asked to have resources for families to engage in this work.

Since the start of the Foundation of Prayer for Priests, people from all walks of life have responded. Elderly women and men in convalescent homes who have discovered a way to contribute to the holiness of priests by offering up their suffering and praying the Rosary for them. Parents of young children have created a prayer oratory at home with pictures of seminarians and priests. By becoming members of the Foundation of Prayer for Priests, they have solidarity with intercessors from fifteen countries. Our Vianney Cenacles have formed in many dioceses. Due to the need, we keep generating online and printed resources, offering conferences, retreats, expanding the mission through four pillars: prayer, sacrifice, service, and study.[31]

The urgency and vision are perennial. This moment is pregnant with promise for you and the Church. Your yes matters to the Lord of the harvest.

---

[31] Foundation of Prayer for Priests mission is to spiritually uphold, protect, and advance the holiness and fruitfulness of the priesthood of the Lord through prayer, sacrifice, service, and study. See www.foundationforpriests.org; inquire at info@ foundationforpriests.org.

Urgency: Why We *Must* Pray for Priests

ᴕ

Lectio

1. "The reason the Son of God appeared was to destroy the works of the devil" (1 John 3:8).

2. "If one member suffers, all suffer together; if one member is honored, all rejoice together" (1 Cor. 12:26).

3. "The harvest is plentiful, but the laborers are few; pray therefore the Lord of the harvest to send out laborers into his harvest" (Luke 10:2).

Meditatio

Jesus to a Benedictine monk: "The renewal of My priesthood in the Church will begin from the fire of love that blazes in the Sacrament of My Body and Blood. I am close to you now, and you are close to Me in the Sacrament of My love. I accept your presence here tonight as an offering of friendship and reparation for the sake of all My priests and brothers. Tonight I look for them. I wait for each one to seek Me out. I continue to yearn that My chosen ones, even those who have allowed their hearts to grow hard against Me, will be converted tonight and find their way to My Tabernacle where I wait for them. Adore Me for the sake of your brother priests who do not adore Me. Let me give you what I would give each of them. Accept My love. Receive My divine friendship."[32]

---

[32] *In Sinu Jesu*, 48-49.

Respond

1. Consider your experience and concept of priesthood, Church, sacraments, prayer, spiritual motherhood or fatherhood. Is there need for healing, forgiveness, correction?

2. Do you feel called to pray more intentionally for priests? Why? How?

3. Do you experience some spiritual warfare in trying to live the call to pray and fast for priests? How do you respond?

St. John Chrysostom's Deliverance Prayer

O Eternal God, you who have redeemed
the race of men from the captivity of the Devil,
deliver me, your servant, from all the workings of unclean
spirits. Command the evil and impure spirits and demons to
depart from your servant and not to remain nor hide in me.
Let them be banished from me, the creation of your hands,
in your holy name, and that of your only-begotten Son,
and of your life-creating Spirit, so that after being cleansed
from all demonic influence, I may live godly, justly, and
righteously and may be counted worthy to receive
the Holy Mysteries of your only-begotten Son
and our God, with whom you are blessed and glorified,
together with the all-holy and good, life-creating Spirit, now
and ever and unto the ages of ages. Amen.[33]

---

[33] Quoted in Paul Thigpen, *Manual of Spiritual Warfare* (Charlotte, NC: Tan Books, 2014), 299.

2

⁂

Mary, Priests, and Spiritual Motherhood

God the Son wishes to form himself,
and, in a manner of speaking,
become incarnate every day in His
members through His dear Mother.[34]
—St. Louis Marie de Montfort

In Mary we find the icon of spiritual motherhood. As the Mother
of God, Mary's "divine maternity" makes her God's sublime
gift to the Church, as expressed beautifully by Fr. Reginald
Garrigou-Lagrange:

> There can be no question of calling her a priest in the
> strict sense of the word since she has not received the
> priestly character and cannot offer Holy Mass nor give
> sacramental absolution. *But . . . her divine maternity is a*
> *greater dignity than the priesthood of the ordained priest in*

---

[34] Quoted in *God Alone: The Collected Writings of St. Louis Ma-*
rie de Montfort (Bayshore, NY: Montfort Publications, 1987),
298.

the sense that it is more to give Our Savior his human nature than to make His body present in the Blessed Eucharist. Mary has given us the Priest of the sacrifice of the Cross, the Principal Priest of the sacrifice of the Mass and the Victim offered on the altar.[35]

Because of her divine maternity, Mary's heart beats with mercy for each priest without exception. Although some priests have no particular devotion to Mary, this does not preclude her devotion to them. Once a young priest admitted that he was not devoted to Mary because he had suffered very much in his lifetime, and he thought Mary could not relate to his suffering because she was preserved from pain by a special grace from God. Only after reading the popular book *33 Days to Morning Glory*[36] did his heart break open to let Mary inside because he learned the extent of Mary's suffering. The priest was transformed when he let Mary into his priesthood for the first time. His strained relationship with his earthly mother was subsequently healed.

Since Mary participated in the immolation of Jesus the High Priest, she understands everything about the priest and assists him in his own process of sanctification. Is the maternal heart of Mary really capable of anything less?

Mary: Mother of Priests

Priests are often referred to as sons of the Virgin Mary. The most joyful priests I have met are those who consecrate themselves

[35] Fr. Reginald Garrigou-Lagrange, O.P., *Mother of the Savior and Our Interior Life* (Charlotte, NC: TAN Books, 1993), 184, emphasis added.

[36] Michael E. Gaitley, M.I.C., *33 Days to Morning Glory* (Stockbridge, MA: Marian Press, 2011).

to Mary and relate to her as a son. She is the *perfect* Mother of all Catholic priests because she is the Mother of the Eternal High Priest.

Fr. Peter Cameron, O.P., explains, "Despite the excellence of our mothers, we persist nonetheless in looking for that *ultimate* maternal mirror in which we can discover ourselves to our deepest depths. Mary's is the face we seek."[37] Why? Pope Benedict XVI explains the reason we need her help: "We can only love ourselves if we have first been loved by someone else. The life a mother gives to her child is not just physical life; she gives total life when she takes the child's tears and turns them into smiles. It is only when life has been accepted and is perceived as accepted that it becomes also acceptable."[38] We can understand now why "Mary's is the face we seek" as the "ultimate maternal mirror" and why she helps us know that we are lovable. In a distinct way Mary does this for priests.

We see a recent and vivid example of Mary's maternity of priests in the pontificate of Pope John Paul II, who chose *Totus tuus* ("totally yours") as his papal motto. When the Polish pope spiritually encountered Mary during the Second World War, he wrote, "I was convinced that Mary leads us to Christ, but at that time I began to realize also that Christ leads us to his mother."[39] Most people are aware that Pope John Paul II credited Mary's intercession for sparing his life when four bullets from a would-be assassin struck him while he was blessing pilgrims in St. Peter's

---

[37] Peter Cameron, O.P., *The Mysteries of the Virgin Mary* (Cincinnati: Servant Books, 2010), 61.

[38] Ibid.

[39] Karl Wojtyla, quoted by Hayden Williams, O.F.M. Cap., *Serving the Love of Loves* (Malta: Outlook Coop., 2011), 174.

Square on May 13, 1981. A year to the day later, the pope placed one of those bullets in Mary's crown at the Shrine of Our Lady of Fátima in Portugal. The Virgin Mary miraculously helped guide the bullets away from vital organs to save the pope's life. Her spiritual motherhood for all clergy is equally active and protective. Only in heaven will we know the many ways in which Mary led and protected us. The would-be assassin's bullet is now a jewel in Our Lady's crown, a testimony to Our Lady of Victory; and no matter how grave a situation is, the final word belongs to God.

The renowned Mariologist Fr. Emile Neubert, S.M., in his wonderful book *Mary and the Priestly Ministry*, helps us to understand Mary's spiritual maternity, which stems from her "cooperation in the mysteries of the Incarnation, the Redemption, and the distribution of grace."[40] Let us note how Mary becomes the Mother of priests:

1. The *Incarnation* sets special grounds for Mary's motherhood of priests. Mary provided the material cause of Christ's priesthood. Mary then carried all her Son's future priests in her womb along with Him. She did not know them individually at that time, but she wished for them what Jesus wished for them at that time, and loved them with the same special love her Son had for them.

2. Our Mother Mary's special role in the *Redemption*: If Mary, in the Incarnation, conceived us spiritually, as it were, then in the mystery of the Redemption she gave us birth. At the foot of the Cross, Christ confided Mary to John, who was a priest, and it is to priests, above all, that

---

[40] Fr. Emile Neubert, S.M., *Mary and the Priestly Ministry* (New Bedford, MA: Academy of the Immaculate, 2009), 8.

Christ gives His Mother because He has a greater love for them and they have a greater need of her.

3. Our Mother Mary's special role in the *distribution of grace*: Mary has a special love for priests: if maternity consists essentially in giving and in nurturing life, can any human maternity be understood apart from such a love? Mary loves all the faithful with incomparable love. But she loves priests with an altogether unique love because she sees in the priest a greater resemblance to the image of her Son than in any other Christian of equal holiness.

Fr. Neubert also gives us five reasons for Mary's special love for priests:

1. She sees in the priest a greater resemblance to the image of her Son than in any other Christian of equal holiness.

2. Jesus loves His priests with a distinctive love. Mary shares all the feeling of her Son.

3. It is thanks to priests, above all, that the work of Christ is carried out in the world.

4. In her union with her Son, she foresaw especially those who would continue His mission on earth.

5. She needs priests. It is especially through them that she can carry out her mission of giving Jesus to the world.[41]

Fr. Neubert's teaching reflects the complementarity of Mary and the priest for God's plan. By extension, Marian spiritual mothers do the same. Alice von Hildebrand wrote: "How

[41] Ibid., 8-17.

beautiful is the complementariness of men and women according to the Divine Plan. It is not by accident that St. Francis of Assisi was best understood by St. Clare; St. Francis of Sales by St. Jeanne Francoise de Chantal; St. Vincent de Paul by Louise de Marillac."[42]

In 2008, Fr. John Cihak gave a presentation entitled "The Blessed Virgin Mary's Role in the Celibate Priest's Spousal and Paternal Love"[43] at Mount St. Mary's Seminary in Emmitsburg, Maryland. It is now distributed to diocesan seminarians and priests who receive instruction at the Institute for Priestly Formation in Omaha, Nebraska. I encourage readers to consult the document online for a better understanding of spiritual motherhood.[44]

Particularly insightful are Fr. Cihak's suggestions regarding the four major dimensions of priestly masculinity and feminine complementarity; they teach the ordered structure of Marian spiritual motherhood.

Fr. Cihak writes:

In the order of nature, we can begin to see the importance of women in the development of the priest as a man: his mother and his sisters help to lead him into maturity as a good son and brother. A man's relationship with his mother begins *in utero* where as son he begins to become

[42] Alice Von Hildebrand, *The Privilege of Being a Woman* (Ann Arbor: Sapientia Press, 2005), 47.

[43] Fr. John Cihak, S.T.D., "The Blessed Virgin Mary's Role in the Celibate Priest's Spousal and Paternal Love," presented at the Bicentennial Marian Symposium at Mount St. Mary's Seminary, Emmitsburg, Maryland, October 9-11, 2008.

[44] This document can be accessed online for free at www.ignatiusinsight.com/features2009/jcihak_maryandpriests1_july09.asp.

attuned to his mother, her heartbeat, her bodily processes, her movements, her emotions; we could say even her soul. In infancy, it is hoped, at some point the mother's smile awakens him to self-consciousness. Her smile gives him his awareness in the midst of her feminine love that he is a unique person. The beauty, goodness, and truth evinced in the mother's smile awakens in the child an awareness of the beauty, goodness, and truth of the world, and by analogy, of God.

Psychiatry and neurobiology describe this as a process of "secure (healthy) attachment," a subtle attunement between mother and child which is essential for normal brain and psychological development, as well as normal spiritual development, especially in those crucial first five years of life. This relationship continues in childhood where a boy continues to learn how to be a son and eventually a brother. In all of this development the mother's (and sisters') role is neither as an object to be used, nor as being overprotective or cultivating a "womanish" affect in her son--all of which would be a collapsing of the masculine-feminine complementarity. The healthy son or brother does not identify with the mother or sister in such a way that he imitates her femininity (e.g., in imitating effeminate characteristics himself); rather, he relates to her as truly an "other" with whom he, in his masculinity, can relate through a process of complementary, self-giving love.

... In the life of grace, we immediately grasp Our Lady's role in helping a man be a good son.

... This complementary engagement of the Blessed Virgin Mary's feminine love with the priest's masculine love happens within the central mystery of the priesthood: the Cross, and specifically in the scene of Our Lady and St. John at the foot of the Cross.[45]

This reminds me of a story I once heard. A very old priest was close to death. Some friends asked a nun from a local convent to help look after the infirm priest, and she cheerfully did so. During her daily visits, she helped the old priest in every way possible, always trying to bring joy to his routine and simply to keep him company. After a few weeks, the priest said to her, "All of my life, I have tried to avoid women, since I am a priest. But in these last weeks that you have visited me, I see that I unnecessarily deprived myself of the grace of friendships that would have enriched my priesthood. But I am grateful to have learned this now, rather than not to have known this gift at all."

That we might better understand and appreciate the essence of spiritual motherhood of priests, we can also reflect upon Jesus's act of entrusting His Mother Mary and John the Beloved to each other. Fr. Cihak, drawing from this scene at the foot of the Cross, continues developing the idea of the complementarity of the feminine heart of Mary, which calls forth the best of the masculine heart of John for their mutual support:

> I like to meditate on that scene, pondering the eyes of Our Lady and St. John as they meet in their mutual agony. Neither of them seems to have Jesus anymore. At that moment she needs St. John; she also allows him to help her. She is so alone at the moment. She who is sinless allows her great poverty of spirit to need this man and priest

---

[45] Cihak, "The Blessed Virgin Mary's Role in the Celibate Priest's Spousal and Paternal Love."

beside her. Her feminine complementarity draws out the best in St. John's masculine heart. The need for his support and protection must have connected to something deep within him as a man. How does he help her? St. John says that he then took her "into his own" (in Greek, *eis ta idia*). What does this mean? "His house," as many translations read? "His things"? What about "everything that he is"? Perhaps it indicates that he takes her into his life as a priest.

She also is supporting him. He is depending on her in that moment for he too is so alone. I wonder if he felt abandoned by the other apostles. She leads the way in sacrificing herself, for her feminine heart is more receptive and more attuned to Jesus's. She is not only present but leads the way for him, helping the priest to have his own heart pierced as well. There is much here to ponder as she engages his masculine love. He gives himself over to her, to cherish her and console her. At this moment she needs him and needs him to be strong, even if she is the one really supporting him.

The Blessed Virgin Mary's role is to call out of the priest this celibate *agape* to help him become a husband to the Church and a spiritual father—a strong father, even in his weakness. She does this at the Cross by drawing the priest out of his own pain to offer pure masculine love in the midst of her own pure feminine love. This scene becomes an icon of the relationship between the priest and the Church. The priest hands himself over to the Church in her suffering and need—to have his life shaped by hers. At the foot of the Cross the Church agonizes in labor to give birth to the members of the mystical body.[46]

This reflection portrays how Mary draws the best out of a priest's masculine heart to guide him to become a strong father for the Church, "even in his weakness." Mary "mothers" a priest to become a husband for the Church by his celibate agape.

The DNA of the Incarnate Word remains with Mary just as the DNA of any child remains with his mother.[47] But Mary's Child is the Eternal High Priest sent by the Father for the redemption of humanity. Mary's heart goes out to the priest because she sees the indelible image of the Eternal High Priest that was conferred upon him by the sacrament of Holy Orders. She who was mystically crucified with Jesus is mystically united to the priest by an act of God's will to which she is completely surrendered.

Mary knows the priest earnestly needs a mother—just as Jesus needed His Mother to fulfill His mission. The Son became dependent upon the Mother's yes at the Incarnation, and the Mother was dependent upon the Son's yes for her redemption. What she did for Jesus on earth she does for the priests who continue the unbroken lineage of the Eternal High Priest. She loves, encourages, protects, feeds, embraces, cleans, delights, teaches, and keeps him company. She who did not leave her Son at the foot of the Cross remains with the priest for his singular mission.

---

[46] Cihak, "The Blessed Virgin Mary's Role in the Celibate Priest's Spousal and Paternal Love."

[47] Nancy Shute, "Beyond Birth: A Child's Cells May Help or Harm the Mother Long after Delivery," *Scientific American*, April 30, 2010, accessed October 15, 2013, www.scientificamerican.com/article.cfm?id=fetal-cells-microchimerism.

Mary, Priests, and Spiritual Motherhood

Mary saw the truth of the Crucifixion, and she knows how to lead the priest to victory through the Cross.

Love compelled the Mother to enter into the sacrifice of the Son so she could experience the mystical crucifixion of each priest chosen to imitate Christ. Mary assists the priest in the refinement of his will, in the purification of his heart, in the conformity of his mind to God. Mary aids the priest in living chastely and growing in charity, wisdom, and fortitude for a martyrdom of love. She who experienced the mystical Crucifixion of Jesus will help each priest to do the same for the joy of the kingdom of God.

The priest needs the love of Mary's feminine heart to bring him to the fulfillment of the masculine ideal in order to protect humanity from all that is harmful. Jesus, the New Adam, is the Redeemer and protector of the human family. The priest is the protector of all that belongs to Christ: men, women, and children, heaven and earth. The priest is at his best when, like Christ, he guards the dignity and vocation of every man, woman, and child.

Mary is God's guardian of the priest's dignity and vocation. The Mother gently moves him to be transfigured into Christ. Through the maternal mediation of Mary, the priest becomes the sacrifice that offers the perfect Sacrifice; the priest becomes the love that offers Love.

Mary: Icon of Spiritual Motherhood

Jesus once made an assertion to Ven. Conchita, a spiritual mother of many priests, and the mother of a priest son: "Priests must go to heaven, and not alone, but with a retinue of souls saved by their conduct; and how many also go to hell dragging many souls condemned by their sin!"[48] Jesus's assertion speaks to the reality of spiritual battle in the life of priests. This is why the Holy See is urgently calling us to strengthen the ministerial priesthood. Matthew's Gospel reminds us: "For it is written, 'I will strike the shepherd, and the sheep of the flock will be scattered'" (Matt. 26:31).

Spiritually placing ourselves and priests under the mantle of Mary is not a magical formula, but it is a remedy for our time when done as part of an authentic consecration to the Immaculate Heart of Mary. In practical terms, it means, "I'm Mary's child." Or as a priest recently said at a conference, "I'm Mary's problem — not my own!" This priest was truly free of himself!

Mary's spiritual motherhood is addressed in the *Catechism*:

> This motherhood of Mary in the order of grace continues uninterruptedly from the consent which she loyally gave at the Annunciation and which she sustained without wavering beneath the cross, until the eternal fulfillment of all the elect. Taken up to heaven she did not lay aside this saving office but by her manifold intercession continues to bring us the gifts of eternal salvation.... Therefore the Blessed Virgin is invoked in the Church under the titles of Advocate, Helper, Benefactress, and Mediatrix.[49]

The mystical piercing of Mary's heart was silent and hidden and was for the sake of an unending joy. The Gospels never record a verbal protest, argument, or any other kind of resistance from the Mother of Jesus. Hers is the perfect imitation of her Son, of whom it is written, "Like a lamb that is led to the slaughter,

---

[48] A Mis Sacerdotes, 111 (text translated by John Nahrgang).
[49] Lumen Gentium, no. 62, quoted in CCC, no. 969.

and like a sheep that before its shearers is dumb, so he opened not his mouth" (Isa. 53:7). With Mary's silence comes all the concentration of her heart to be completely surrendered. Her broken heart becomes a portal through which St. John and every priest thereafter can enter to receive the consolation of Marian charity and strength.

The silence and sorrow of the feminine heart of Mary are one dimension of a holy mother's heart. Another powerful dimension is joy and praise, which forever resonate in her immaculate being. We know that Mary's Magnificat hymn of praise was not a singular outburst of uncontainable gratitude; rather, it is her perpetual anthem of love to the Trinity. Therefore, Mary's feminine, maternal heart is for us a school of servanthood for priests and spiritual mothers or fathers of clergy. Christlike servanthood includes sorrows and joys, silence and proclamation. Mary teaches us to be anchored in grateful service to God and the Church.

The test of authentic motherhood is fruitful service, not selfish covetousness. Motherhood is about remembering to be true to the feminine ideal of *receptivity* that always makes room for the other. These terms sound very sacrificial, and they are. But every mother learns that the travail of birthing something beautiful is worth it! It is a matter of love that flowers naturally like a rose that is rooted in earthly soil but blooms by sunlight and water. A mother's love grows out of the feminine heart attuned to the Sacred and Immaculate Hearts. The feminine heart needs to drink deeply of divine love to become a living spring like Mary's.

The greatest of all maternal loves is that of the Virgin Mary, Mother of Jesus! Mary's maternal love always magnifies the Lord, always proclaims His marvelous deeds, always remembers what God has done and always rejoices in being chosen to serve. I believe Mary's perpetual *Magnificat* is a hymn she desires to inscribe on the heart of every believer so that the Church may form one united chorus of praise and gratitude, affirming, "He has mercy on those who fear him in every generation" (Luke 1:46-55). The motherhood of Mary is always fruitful in service to the glory of God. She is our heavenly Mother, perpetually engaged in forming other mothers to whom life can be entrusted—physical and spiritual—because maternal love is always abundantly creative.

Another icon of Mary's motherhood that is greatly venerated, especially in the Americas, is Our Lady of Guadalupe. Her iconic words to St. Juan Diego reflect a sublime and merciful maternal love:

> Hear and understand, my smallest and dearest son, that what is alarming and afflicting you is nothing. Do not let your countenance or your heart be disturbed. Do not fear this illness or any other illness or suffering. Am I, your Mother, not here? Are you not under my shadow and protection? Am I not the source of your joy? Are you not in the folds of my mantle, in the crossing of my arms? What more do you need?[50]

These words are a healing balm for every child of Mary. Who are the children of Mary? God gave Mary to *all His children*! In Mary, everyone finds the perfect maternal love that brings out the best in us.

But there is a deeper way of abiding in the Immaculate Heart—through Marian consecration. St. Louis de Montfort

---

[50] Our Lady of Guadalupe to Juan Diego, quoted in Paul Badde, *María of Guadalupe: Shaper of History, Shaper of Hearts* (San Francisco: Ignatius Press, 2008), 33-34.

and St. Maximilian Kolbe have spread the glories of Marian consecration throughout the Church.[51] Pope Pius XII defines consecration in this way:

> Consecration to the Mother of God is a total gift of self, for the whole of life and for all eternity; and a gift which is not a mere formality or sentimentality, but effectual, comprising the full intensity of the Christian life — Marian life. This consecration tends essentially to union with Jesus, under the guidance of Mary.[52]

The work of Christ in the Church is always magnified through the heart of Mary. To live Marian consecration is to live Christ, since their two hearts are bound in one love.

We have been given a great confirmation of the efficacy of Marian consecration in recent times through Pope Francis's consecration of the entire world to Mary on October 13, 2013. When the Vicar of Christ dedicates the world to Mary, it reflects a great need for maternal intervention to help us reorder our lives to God.

Who doesn't need the Mother of God to advocate for him? And who would choose to live without the consolation of Mary's company and help? And who would refuse to join in her maternal mission of saving souls? To be consecrated to Mary is to be set apart for a sacred purpose. One who is set apart for a

---

[51] Two wonderful contemporary books on Marian consecration are Fr. Michael Gaitley's *33 Days to Morning Glory* (Stockbridge, MA: Marian Press, 2011) and Fr. Brian McMaster's *Totus Tuus: A Consecration to Jesus through Mary with Blessed John Paul II* (Huntington, IN: Our Sunday Visitor, 2013).

[52] Pope Pius XII, Consecration to the Immaculate Heart of Mary, October 31, 1942.

sacred purpose is under the mantle of grace. A holy alliance, a covenant, is forged when a person offers himself to God through Mary. A covenant is a profound reality in the spiritual realm. A communion exists between Mary and her consecrated children so she can act freely and gloriously on their behalf.

But Mary never acts independently of her Spouse, the Holy Spirit. Yes, God willed that Mary and the Holy Spirit be espoused. The great St. Louis de Montfort helps us to understand the significance of this:

> To Mary his faithful spouse, God the Holy Spirit has communicated his unspeakable gifts; and he has chosen her to be the dispenser of all he possesses, in such wise that she distributes to whom she wills, as much as she wills, as she wills and when she wills, all his gifts and graces. The Holy Spirit gives no heavenly gift to men which he does not have pass through her virginal hands. Such has been the will of God, who has willed that we should have everything through Mary; so that she who, impoverished, humbled, and who hid herself even unto the abyss of nothingness by her profound humility her whole life long, should now be enriched and exalted and honored by the Most High. Such are the sentiments of the Church and holy Fathers.[53]

Since this book deals with the sanctification of priests, and the laity who pray for them, it is important to understand how Mary and the Holy Spirit work together to sanctify souls. Jesus was conceived by the Holy Spirit and born of the Virgin Mary. We know this since it is part of our Creed.

---

[53] St. Louis de Montfort, *True Devotion to Mary*, no. 25.

Mary, Priests, and Spiritual Motherhood

Archbishop Luis María Martínez teaches:

That is the way Jesus is always conceived. That is the way He is reproduced in souls. He is always the fruit of Heaven and earth. Two artisans — the Holy Spirit and the most holy Virgin Mary — must concur in the work that is at once God's masterpiece and humanity's supreme product. Both the Holy Spirit and the Virgin Mary are necessary to souls, for they are the only ones who can reproduce Christ....

These two, then, the Holy Spirit and Mary, are the indispensable artificers of Jesus, the indispensable sanctifiers of souls. Any saint in Heaven can cooperate in the sanctification of a soul, but his cooperation is not necessary, not profound, not constant. But the cooperation of these two artisans of Jesus of whom we have just been speaking is so necessary that, without it, souls are not sanctified (and this by the actual design of Providence), and so intimate that it reaches to the very depths of our soul.... Such is the place that the Holy Spirit and the Virgin Mary have in the order of sanctification.[54]

Archbishop Martínez helps us to understand that we need to invoke Mary *and* the Holy Spirit, since they are the two artisans who conceive Jesus in a soul. Mary and the Holy Spirit *always* work together. The sanctification of priests is *their joint mission.*

---

[54] Luis M. Martínez, *True Devotion to the Holy Spirit* (Manchester, NH: Sophia Institute Press, 2000), 8-9. Archbishop Martínez was Archbishop of Mexico from 1937 until his death in 1956.

Mary's spiritual motherhood of humanity did not begin at the foot of the Cross when Jesus said to John, "Behold, your Mother" (John 19:27). Mary's spiritual maternity began when the Holy Spirit overshadowed her at the Incarnation, according to Fr. Neubert, who states, "In the mystery of the Incarnation, Mary becomes the Mother of all the faithful, because in giving life to our Head, she simultaneously gave it to all the members of the Mystical Body of Christ."[55]

Spiritual Motherhood of Priests

In this book, it is my ardent desire to encourage women to live spiritual motherhood of priests in union with Mary. St. Edith Stein (also known by her religious name, Teresa Benedicta of the Cross) describes how this is possible:

The *intrinsic value of woman* consists essentially in *exceptional receptivity for God's work in the soul.*[56]

For an understanding of our unique feminine nature, let us look to the pure love and spiritual maternity of Mary. This spiritual maternity is the core of a woman's soul. Wherever a woman functions authentically in this spirit of maternal pure love, Mary collaborates with her. This holds true whether the woman is married or single, professional or domestic or both, a Religious in the world or in the convent. Through this love, a woman is God's special weapon in His fight against evil. Her intrinsic value is that she is able to do so because she has a special susceptibility

---

[55] *Mary and the Priestly Ministry*, 10.
[56] St. Edith Stein, *Essays on Woman* (Washington, D.C.: ICS Publications, 1996), 259.

for the works of God in souls—her own and others. She relates to others in His spirit of love.[57]

Here St. Edith Stein helps women understand that the feminine heart in union with Mary's is a formidable defense against evil. Women are created to be life-givers and life-savers. The vocation to life and love is always opposed to death and evil. The Scriptures are vivid lessons on spiritual battles. Daughters (and sons) of Mary are in the Queen Mother's army to fight against evil. "The war on maternity is a crime whose horror threatens the future of humanity and is in fact a satanic attack on Mary," wrote Gertrude von le Fort.[58]

Edith Stein develops spiritual maternity here, "Everywhere the need exists for maternal sympathy and help, and thus we are able to recapitulate in the one word motherliness that which we have developed as the characteristic value of woman. Only, the motherliness must be that which does not remain within the narrow circle of blood relations or of personal friends; but in accordance with the model of the Mother of Mercy, it must have its root in universal divine love for *all* who are there, belabored and burdened."

Most would agree that clergy are among the most belabored and burdened. Will we make room in our hearts to carry them spiritually and present them daily to the Lord?

A very feminine image comes to me now: that of a pregnant womb. I think the feminine heart is something like that when it is exercising maternal love—it expands to include

---

[57] St. Edith Stein, quoted by Freda Mary Oben in *The Life and Thought of St. Edith Stein* (New York: Alba House, 2001), 82.

[58] Gertrude von le Fort, *The Eternal Woman* (San Francisco: Ignatius Press, 2010), ix.

everyone who needs her love. As St. Edith Stein teaches, this is because women have a "special susceptibility for the works of God in souls — hers and others." Women have a God-given spiritual intuition ordered to the work of divine love. God created women to be life-bearers, and this is a distinct dignity. Whether the life we bear is spiritual or physical, or both, we are called to be bearers of the Word of God for others in emulation of Mary.

The Church recognizes the need for spiritual motherhood and acknowledges the unique dignity of the maternal-feminine heart. On December 8, 1965, at the closing of the Second Vatican Council, the Council Fathers said, "At this moment when the human race is undergoing so deep a transformation, women impregnated with the spirit of the Gospel can do much to aid mankind in not falling." The word *impregnated* is not accidental. It indicates that women allow the gospel to take hold of their hearts and take root in their minds so as to be able to give the gift they have received to others. This sounds like a tall order! But let us recall St. Edith Stein's words: "Wherever a woman functions authentically in this spirit of maternal pure love, Mary collaborates with her." We have God's Mother to "mother" us in the art of spiritual motherhood.

Mary is always at the service of God and His people, especially His priests. The Congregation for the Clergy's initiative of spiritual maternity rightly points out that the spiritual motherhood of priests is "a hidden vocation, invisible to the naked eye."[59] They invite women disciples to imitate Mary in her maternal motherhood. I know holy women to whom priests

[59] *Eucharistic Adoration for the Sanctification of Priests and Spiritual Maternity*, 12.

confide their deep need for prayer. Not a word is ever spoken to anyone about this while the spiritual mother prays and suffers for the priest's intention, winning grace for his priesthood. This is authentic spiritual motherhood of priests. The charism of spiritual maternity of priests can be a vocation within a vocation and can be lived by people of all walks of life.

A woman who is called to spiritual maternity of priests should first be schooled in the virtues of the Mother of the Eternal High Priest. She must be thoroughly Marian in character, thought, word, and deed. She should have spent hours of reflection with Mary to learn from her how to pray for priests — never assuming that she knows how to pray, but always aware that she must be led by the Holy Spirit, who led Mary to pray and serve.

To the priest, she should bring the face and heart of Mary and no other agenda. It was Mary's self-effacement that made it possible for her to magnify the Lord.

The Congregation for the Clergy's booklet teaches:

> The vocation to be a spiritual mother for priests is largely unknown, scarcely understood and, consequently, rarely lived, notwithstanding its fundamental importance. It is a vocation that is frequently hidden, invisible to the naked eye, but meant to transmit spiritual life....
>
> The present situation of the Church in a secularized world and the subsequent crisis of faith has the pope, bishops, priests, and faithful looking for a way forward. At the same time, it is becoming increasingly clear that the real solution lies in the interior renewal of priests, and in this context the so-called "spiritual maternity of priests" assumes a special role. Through being "spiritual

mothers", women and mothers participate in the universal motherhood of Mary, who as mother of the Supreme and Eternal High Priest, is also the mother of all priests of all times.

If in natural life a child is conceived, born, nurtured and cared for by its mother, then this applies even more to the spiritual life: behind all priests there is a spiritual mother who asked God for their vocation. She bears them through spiritual suffering and "nourishes" them by offering to God all her daily activities, so that they become holy priests, priests faithful to their special identity and special commitments.[60]

The booklet *Eucharistic Adoration for the Sanctification of Priests and Spiritual Maternity* emphasizes several crucial points about the priesthood and women in the Church:

- The Church's way forward in addressing a crisis of faith in a secularized world is through *the interior renewal of priests.*

- *Women participate in the universal motherhood of Mary.*

- "Spiritual maternity of priests" assumes a special role in this renewal.

- A spiritual mother bears priests through spiritual suffering and "nourishes" them by offering to God all her prayers and sufferings and even her ordinary daily activities.

---

[60] Ibid., 12-13.

- A spiritual mother thus helps them become holy priests who are faithful to their special identity.

Women who choose Mary as their model of discipleship will become like our Mother in fruitfulness through *obedient* service to the Church, beginning with praying for priests.

�֎

SPIRITUAL EXERCISE

Lectio

1. "For it is written, 'I will strike the shepherd, and the sheep of the flock will be scattered'" (Matt. 26:31).

2. "And Mary said, 'Behold, I am the handmaid of the Lord; let it be to me according to your word'" (Luke 1:38).

3. "Behold, your Mother" (John 19:27).

Meditatio

Mary teaches us how to be a mother to souls. She is a Mother who understands sorrow and can empathize with it perfectly, who consoles and encourages, who sacrifices herself without holding back, who finds it natural to live only for her children, giving them herself and all that she has without looking for any return. The Church is a mother, and priests represent this mother-Church in the eyes of the faithful. Mary can instill in their hearts her own maternal love.[61]

---

[61] Fr. Emile Neubert, SM, *Mary and the Priestly Ministry* (New Bedford, MA: Franciscans of the Immaculate, 2009), 170.

Praying for Priests

Respond

1. Consider how many people have drifted away from the practice of the Faith, and you remain steadfast. How and why?

2. Consider how you relate to priests in your life. What thoughts arise?

3. How have Mary and her priests influenced your vocation?

Prayer for Priests by St. John Vianney

God, please give to your Church today
many more priests after your own heart.
May they be worthy representatives of
Christ the Good Shepherd.
May they wholeheartedly devote themselves
to prayer and penance; be examples of humility,
and poverty; shining models of holiness;
tireless and powerful preachers of the Word of God;
zealous dispensers of your grace in the sacraments.
May their loving devotion to your Son Jesus
in the Eucharist and to Mary his Mother
be the twin fountains of fruitfulness
in their ministry. Amen.

3

༄

Spiritual Motherhood in Church History

In the history of the Church, even from earliest times,
there were side-by-side with men a number of women,
for whom the response of the Bride to the Bridegroom's
redemptive love acquired full expressive force.[62]
—St. John Paul II

The saints who lived the vocation of spiritual maternity teach us the beauty of interceding for our shepherds. Women of faith have greatly enriched the Church by spiritually adopting priests. In the previous chapter, we learned that a priest's spiritual mother must first be a daughter of Mary. Now we will learn through the example of other spiritual mothers. Following are profiles of both well-known and unsung heroines who model the charism of spiritual maternity of priests.

St. Faustina Kowalska (1905-1938): religious sister

Known as the "Apostle of Divine Mercy," St. Faustina Kowalska wrote this story about a priest in her spiritual diary:

[62] *Mulieris Dignitatem*, no. 27.

On one occasion I saw a servant of God in the immediate danger of committing a mortal sin. I started to beg God to deign to send down upon me all the torments of hell and all the sufferings He wished if only this priest would be set free and snatched from the occasion of committing a sin. Jesus heard my prayer and, that very instant, I felt a crown of thorns on my head. The thorns penetrated my head with great force right into my brain. This lasted for three hours; the servant of God was set free from this sin, and his soul was strengthened by a special grace of God.[63]

God so loved the priest who was going to fall into sin that He inspired a humble nun to make an offering of herself on behalf of this shepherd! The measure of St. Faustina's charity for priests seemed boundless, but it was costly. On another occasion, a priest (her spiritual director), asked her to pray for him. She replied that she would pray and asked a mortification. When she received permission for a certain mortification, she wrote:

I felt a great desire to give up all the graces that God's goodness intended for me that day in favor of that priest, and I asked the Lord Jesus to deign to bestow upon me, all the sufferings and afflictions, both interior and exterior, that the priest would have to suffer that day. God partially answered my request and, at once, all sorts of difficulties and adversities sprang up out of nowhere. But that was not all: I began to experience interior sufferings. First, I was seized by depression and aversion towards the sisters, then a kind of uncertainty began to trouble me. I could not

[63] *Diary of St. Maria Faustina Kowalska: Divine Mercy in My Soul* (Stockbridge: Marian Press, 1987), no. 41.

recollect myself during prayer, and various things would take hold of my mind. Then I heard in my soul a voice, saying, "My daughter, why are you weeping? After all, you yourself offered to undertake these sufferings. Know that what you have taken upon yourself for that soul is only a small portion. He is suffering much more." And I asked the Lord, "Why are You treating him like that?" The Lord answered me that it was for the triple crown meant for him: that of virginity, the priesthood and martyrdom. At that moment, a great joy flooded my soul at the sight of the great glory that is going to be his in heaven. I said the "Te Deum" for this special grace of God: namely, of learning how God treats those He intends to have close to himself. (*Diary*, no. 596)

St. Monica (331-387): laywoman, wife, and mother

St. Monica is a famous example of a mother's fifteen years of intercession for her son, through tears, prayers, and laments. And she kept peace in her family by quelling her husband's rages with kindness. After his radical conversion, St. Augustine praised his mother's untiring intercession with words of ardent charity: "For love of me, she cried more tears than a mother would over the bodily death of her son. Nine years passed in which I wallowed in the slime of that deep pit and the darkness of falsehood. Yet that pious widow desisted not all the hours of her supplications, to bewail my case unto Thee where her prayers entered into Thy presence."[64]

---

[64] St. Augustine, quoted in *Eucharistic Adoration for the Sanctification of Priests and Spiritual Maternity*, 11.

Augustine said thankfully, "My holy mother never abandoned me. She brought me forth in her flesh that I might be born to this temporal light, and in her heart, that I might be born to life eternal. I have my mother to thank for what I have become and the way that I arrived there!"[65] Through the ages, Catholic mothers and wives have taken St. Monica as their patron and inspiration. I implored her help quite often in the raising of my sons and was always strengthened by her example.

St. Catherine of Siena (1347-1380): single laywoman

Catherine was holy from her youth, and at the age of six she had a mystical experience of Jesus that forever changed her life. Her maternal love embraced priests through her constant intercession for them. She even became a spiritual mother to Pope Gregory XI, and in 1376 she persuaded him to move the entire Papal Court back to Rome from Avignon, France. In early March 1376, she wrote to Pope Gregory XI:

> I tell you in the name of Christ crucified that you must use your authority.... You are in charge of the garden of the holy Church. So [first of all] uproot from that garden the stinking weeds filled of impurity and avarice, and bloated with pride (I mean the evil pastors and administrators who poison and corrupt the garden).... Use your authority, you who are in charge of us! Uproot these weeds and throw them out where they will have nothing to administer! Tell them to tend to administering themselves by a good holy life. Plant fragrant flowers in this garden for us, pastors and administrators who will be true servants of

---

[65] Ibid., 15.

Jesus Christ crucified, who will seek only God's honor and the salvation of souls, who will be fathers to the poor.[66]

In late March 1376, Catherine wrote to a cardinal: "I say you are a pillar to keep this bride's home safe. So you must be strong, not weak; for weak things topple with the slightest wind—whether that wind is difficulty, or some wrong that may be done to us, or too much of the world's abundance and prosperity, pleasure and grandeur."[67]

She was a spiritual mother for other priests also. On one occasion, Catherine wrote the following to the Dominican friar Bl. Raymond of Capua, her spiritual director:

I've heard ... that you have been experiencing tremendous struggles and that your spirit has been overtaken by darkness because of the devil's illusions and deceits. He wants to make you see the crooked as straight and the straight as crooked, and he does this to make you stumble along the way so you won't reach your goal. But take heart. God has provided and will continue to provide for you, and his providence will not fail you. See that in everything you turn to Mary as you embrace the cross. And don't ever give in to spiritual discouragement, but navigate the stormy sea on the ship of divine mercy.[68]

---

[66] Quoted in Kathryn Jean Lopez, "What St. Catherine of Siena Would Say to Today's Bishops," Angelus, August 14, 2018, https://angelusnews.com/voices/kathryn-jean-lopez/what-st-catherine-of-siena-would-say-to-todays-bishops.

[67] Ibid.

[68] The Letters of Catherine of Siena, vol. II, trans. Suzanne Noffke (Tempe, AZ: Medieval & Renaissance Studies, 2001), 473.

St. Catherine died at the age of thirty-three and was declared a Doctor of the Church[69] in 1970 by Pope Paul VI.

Eliza Vaughan (d. 1853): laywoman, wife, and mother

Eliza Vaughan came from a strong Protestant family, which helped found the Rolls-Royce car company. Yet even during her childhood education in France, she was deeply impressed by the exemplary efforts of the Catholic Church in caring for the poor.

After she married Colonel John Francis Vaughan in the summer of 1830, Eliza converted to the Catholic Faith, despite the objection of her relatives. During the Catholic persecution in England under Queen Elizabeth I (1558-1603), the Vaughans' ancestors preferred imprisonment and expropriation to being unfaithful to their beliefs.

During the decades of terror in England, Courtfield, the ancestral family home, became a refuge for priests, a place where the Holy Mass was often celebrated secretly.

So profound and zealous was Eliza's religious conversion that she proposed to her husband to offer all of their children back to God. This remarkable woman made a habit of praying for an hour each day before the Blessed Sacrament in the house chapel at Courtfield. She prayed to God for a large family and for many religious vocations among her children. And her prayers were answered! She bore fourteen children and died shortly after the birth of the last child, John, in 1853.

Of the thirteen children who lived, six of her eight boys became priests; two priests in religious orders, one diocesan priest,

---

[69] This honor has been awarded by the Church to only thirty-five individuals for making great contributions to Catholic doctrine or theology.

a bishop, an archbishop, and a cardinal. Of her five daughters, four became nuns in religious orders. What a blessing for the family, and what an impact on all of England!

Two months after Eliza's death, Colonel Vaughan wrote in a letter that he was convinced divine providence had brought Eliza to him: "I thanked the Lord in adoration today that I could give back to him my dearly beloved wife. I poured out my heart to him, full of thankfulness that, as an example and a guide, he gave me Eliza with whom I am still now bound by an inseparable, spiritual bond. What wonderful consolation and grace she brought me! I still see her as I always saw her before the Blessed Sacrament: her inner purity and extraordinary human kindness which her beautiful face reflected during prayer."[70]

St. Thérèse of Lisieux (1873-1897): religious sister

The Little Flower, as St. Thérèse is lovingly called, is a renowned spiritual mother of priests. One of my favorite books, *Maurice and Thérèse: The Story of a Love*, contains the inspiring letters between a struggling young priest and Thérèse. Sr. Thérèse once wrote the following to Fr. Maurice while he was out in the mission fields:

It must be that you don't know me at all well, if you are afraid that a detailed account of your faults could lessen the tenderness that I feel for your soul! O my brother, believe me that I shall not need to "put my hand over the mouth of Jesus," He has forgotten your infidelities long ago. Only your desires for perfection remain to make His heart rejoice.

[70] *Eucharistic Adoration for the Sanctification of Priests and Spiritual Maternity*, 18-19.

I implore you, don't drag yourself to His feet ever again. Follow that first impulse which draws you into His arms."[71]

We can imagine the consolation this message brought! Here is the genius of Thérèse—complete confidence in God's love and mercy.

The Congregation's booklet highlights a story from her life that reveals the depths of a love ready to suffer for priests:

On a pilgrimage to Rome, when she was only fourteen years old, Thérèse came to understand her vocation to be a spiritual mother for priests. In her autobiography she describes that after meeting many holy priests on her trip to Italy, she understood their weaknesses and frailty in spite of their sublime dignity. *"If holy priests . . . show in their conduct their extreme need for prayers, what is to be said of those who are tepid?"* In one of her letters she encouraged her sister Céline, *"Let us live for souls, let us be apostles, let us save especially the souls of priests . . . let us pray, let us suffer for them, and, on the last day, Jesus will be grateful."*

In the life of Thérèse, Doctor of the Church, there is a moving episode which highlights her zeal for priests, especially missionaries. While she was very ill and had great difficulty walking, the nurse advised her to take a little walk in the garden for a quarter of an hour each day. She obeyed faithfully, although she did not find it effective. On one occasion, the sister accompanying her noticed how painful it was for her to walk and remarked, *"You would do better to rest; this walking can do you no good under such conditions.*

---

[71] Patrick Ahern, *Maurice and Thérèse: The Story of a Love* (New York: Image Books, 1998), 188-189.

You're exhausting yourself." The saint responded, *"Well, I am walking for a missionary. I think that over there, far away, one of them is perhaps exhausted in his apostolic endeavors, and, to lessen his fatigue, I offer mine to God."*[72]

Thérèse's heart, aflame with divine love, intercedes for all souls but especially for priests. These words from young Fr. Maurice, written to his beloved Sr. Thérèse near the time of her death, demonstrate the impact of her maternal heart:

> Let us adore God, Sister. Thank Him with me. This love of God almost scares me. Nonetheless I hope that confidence will win out and make me give myself completely. This above all is asked of me. My spiritual Father has said to me: "You must give yourself completely to God, Who asks that you give Him everything. You cannot serve Him by halves. You will either be a good priest or you will never amount to anything." That is my own feeling, and I want to give without counting the cost, being very sure that "when somebody loves he does not calculate," so that when I set foot on the soil of Africa I'll be able to continue with the words: "I have given all. I run with a light heart. I have nothing anymore except my only riches, namely, To Live by Love."[73]

Venerable Conchita of Mexico (1862-1937): wife, mother of a priest, foundress

The Congregation for the Clergy wrote, "In the future, she will be of great importance for the universal Church. The

---

[72] *Eucharistic Adoration for the Sanctification of Priests and Spiritual Maternity*, 34.
[73] *Maurice and Thérèse*, 117-118.

spiritual motherhood for the sanctification of priests consumed her completely until she died at the age of seventy-five."[74] Concepción (Conchita) Cabrera de Armida, soon to be beatified,[75] was a wife and the mother of nine children (four died in their youth), including a Jesuit priest. Upon the death of her husband, she founded a religious order that still exists. Spending many hours in Eucharistic adoration, she received messages from the Lord regarding the priesthood. These are Church approved and published in the Congregation for the Clergy's booklet also. The Lord explained to her the nature of spiritual maternity:

> There are souls, who through ordination receive a priestly anointing. However, there are ... also priestly souls who do not have the dignity or the ordination of a priest, yet have a priestly mission. They offer themselves united to me.... These souls help the Church in a very powerful spiritual way.... You will be the mother of a great number of spiritual children, yet they will cost your heart the death of a thousand martyrs.
>
> Bring yourself as an offering for the priests. Unite your offering with my offering, to obtain graces for them.... I want to come again into this world ... in my priests. I want to renew the world by revealing myself through the priests. I want give my Church a powerful impulse in which I will pour out the Holy Spirit over my priests like a new Pentecost. The Church and the world need a new

[74] Ibid., 28.
[75] "Pope Clears Seven Candidates for Sainthood and Beatification," Vatican News, June 9, 2018, https://www.vaticannews.va/en/pope/news/2018-06/pope-francis-decrees-canonization-beatification.html.

Pentecost, a priestly Pentecost, an interior Pentecost. I
will entrust to you a different martyrdom, you will suffer
what the priests undertake against me. You will experience and offer up their infidelity and wretchedness.[76]

One of Conchita's sons became a priest. Of him she wrote,
"Manuel was born in the same hour that Fr. Jose Camacho died.
Upon hearing the news, I prayed that my son would replace
him at the altar. When little Manuel began to talk, we prayed
together for the great grace of a vocation to the priesthood. At
the age of seventeen, he joined the Society of Jesus."

In 1914 she met Manuel in Spain for the last time, since he
never returned to Mexico. He wrote in a letter to her, "My dear
little mother, you have shown me the way. Fortunately, I have
heard from your lips since my earliest years the challenging and
saving teaching of the Cross. Now I want to put it into practice."
Imagine his mother's joy and gratitude!

The Mothers of Lu

The little village of Lu, in northern Italy, is located in a rural
area 90 kilometers east of Turin. It would still be unknown to
this day if some of the mothers of Lu had not made a decision
that had important consequences in 1881.

The deepest desire of many of these mothers was for one of
their sons to become a priest or for a daughter to place her life
completely in God's service. Under the direction of their parish priest, Msgr. Alessandro Canora, they gathered every Tues-
day for adoration of the Blessed Sacrament, asking the Lord for

---

[76] Jesus to Conchita, quoted in *Eucharistic Adoration for the Sanctification of Priests and Spiritual Maternity*, 28-29.

vocations. They received Holy Communion on the first Sunday
of every month with the same intention. After Mass, all the
mothers prayed this prayer together:

O God, grant that one of my sons
may become a priest! I myself want to live
as a good Christian and want to guide my children
always to do what is right, so that I may
receive the grace, O God, to be allowed to
give you a holy priest! Amen.

Through the trusting prayer of these mothers, and the open-
ness of the other parents, an atmosphere of deep joy and Christian piety developed in the families, making it much easier for
the children to recognize their vocations. Still, no one expected
that God would hear the prayers of these mothers in such a
dramatic way.

From the tiny village of Lu came 323 vocations: 152 priests
(diocesan and religious) and 171 nuns belonging to forty-one
Congregations. In some cases, several vocations came from a
single family. The most famous example is the Rinaldi family,
from whom God called seven children. Two daughters became
Salesian sisters, both of whom were sent to San Domingo as
missionaries. Five sons became priests, all joining the Salesians.[77]

Servant of God Consolata Betrone
(1903-1946): religious sister

The sacrifices and prayers of a spiritual mother for priests
benefit especially those who have strayed or abandoned their

---

[77] Ibid., 22-23.

vocations. Jesus has called countless women in His Church to this vocation of prayer, such as Sr. Consolata Betrone, a Capuchin nun from Turin. Jesus said to her, "Your lifelong task is for your brothers. Consolata, you, too, shall be a good shepherdess and go in search of your brothers and bring them back to me."

Consolata offered everything for "her brother" priests and others consecrated to God who were in spiritual need. While working in the kitchen, she prayed continuously in her heart, *"Jesus, Mary, I love you; save souls!"* She consciously made every little service and duty into a sacrifice. Jesus said in this regard, "Your duties may be insignificant, but because you bring them to me with such love, I give them immeasurable value and shower them on the discontented brothers as grace for conversion."

Very grave and difficult cases were often entrusted to the prayers of the convent. Consolata would take the corresponding suffering upon herself. For weeks or months on end, she sometimes endured dryness of spirit, abandonment, meaninglessness, inner darkness, loneliness, doubt, and the sinful state of the priests.

She once wrote to her spiritual director during these struggles, "How much the brothers cost me!" Yet Jesus made her a magnificent promise: "Consolata, it is not only one brother that you will lead back to God, but all of them. I promise you, you will give me the brothers, one after another." And so it was! She brought back all of the priests entrusted to her to a fulfilling priesthood. There are recorded testimonies of many of these cases.[78]

---

[78] *Eucharistic Adoration for the Sanctification of Priests and Spiritual Maternity*, 25.

Praying for Priests

Bl. Alexandrina da Costa (1904-1955):
single laywoman

A story from the life of Alexandrina da Costa, beatified on April 25, 2004, reveals the transforming power and visible effects of the sacrifice made by a sick and forgotten girl.

In 1941, Alexandrina wrote to her spiritual director, Fr. Mariano Pinho, telling him that Jesus told her, "My daughter, a priest living in Lisbon is close to being lost forever; he offends me terribly. Call your spiritual director and ask his permission that I may have you suffer in a special way for this soul."

Once Alexandrina had received permission from her spiritual director, she suffered greatly. She felt the severity of the priest's errors, how he wanted to know nothing of God and was close to self-damnation. She even heard the priest's full name. Poor Alexandrina experienced the hellish state of this priest's soul and prayed urgently, "Not to hell, no! I offer myself as a sacrifice for him, as long as you want."

Fr. Pinho inquired of the cardinal of Lisbon whether one of the priests of his diocese was of particular concern. The cardinal openly confirmed that he was, in fact, very worried about one of his priests, and when he mentioned the name of the priest, it was the same name that Jesus had spoken to Alexandrina.

Some months later, a friend of Fr. Pinho, Fr. David Novais, recounted to him an unusual incident. Fr. David had just held a retreat in Fátima, and one of the attendees was a modest gentleman whose exemplary behavior made him pleasantly attractive to all the participants. On the last night of the retreat, this man suddenly had a heart attack. He asked to see a priest, to whom he confessed and received Holy Communion. Shortly thereafter he died, fully reconciled with God. It turned out that this man was actually a priest—the very priest for whom Alexandrina had suffered so greatly.[79]

Mother Judith Zuniga, O.C.D.: Mother Superior of the Carmelite Sisters of the Most Sacred Heart of Los Angeles

In our midst we have many women religious sisters who exemplify spiritual motherhood of priests. I am grateful for Mother Judith Zuniga's testimony, which she graciously wrote at my request. Thank you, Mother, for enriching our understanding of the Church's history of spiritual maternity in the Carmelite family.

How does one begin to verbalize a matter of the heart such as the spiritual maternity of priests? As a Carmelite Sister, I treasure it from the core of my being as a sacred gift that has been entrusted to me.

The realities of spiritual paternity and spiritual maternity are inextricably grounded in the sacrament of Baptism, since, by virtue of our Baptism in Christ, we are made collaborators in His plan of redemption for the salvation of souls.

A baptized Catholic who is genuinely serious about his relationship with Jesus Christ must necessarily cultivate an interior life of prayer in order for this friendship (or bond) to grow and deepen. Charity, good example, and self-sacrifice for the material and spiritual well-being of others are concrete expressions of the fruitfulness of genuine prayer and a loving union with Christ. Thus, a true disciple of Jesus Christ must be attentive to nurturing and strengthening the spiritual life of others. There can be

---

[79] Ibid., 24.

no genuine interior life or sanctity in a soul in which the actualization of spiritual paternity or spiritual maternity is lacking.

In the Gospel of Matthew, Christ tells us that "whoever does the will of my Father in heaven is my brother, and sister, and mother" (12:50). In explaining this passage, Pope John Paul II noted that our Lord wanted us to understand that motherhood "is always related to the Covenant which God established with the human race through the motherhood of the Mother of God." Then, with specific reference to motherhood, the Holy Father stated, "The motherhood of every woman, understood in the light of the Gospel, is similarly not only 'of flesh and blood': it expresses a profound 'listening to the word of the living God' and a readiness to 'safeguard' this Word, which is 'the word of eternal life' (cf. Jn 6:68)."[80]

A spiritual mother, like Mary, is always ready at any cost to safeguard the word of God. In this way, she becomes a personification of Mary, the Mother of God. A spiritual mother, through her own sacrifices, prayers, and works of charity for the sanctification of others, acts *in persona Matris*. A spiritual mother must have not only a profound union with Christ, but also a deeply personal relationship with His beloved Mother. Indeed, spiritual motherhood is truly a very lofty vocation offered to all baptized women who wholeheartedly live out their baptismal consecration.

Spiritual maternity toward priests in particular is profoundly Marian. Just as Mary was devoted to Her Son, the Great High Priest, so, too, spiritual mothers after her own

[80] Pope John Paul II, *Mulieris Dignitatem*, no. 19.

heart are particularly solicitous for the spiritual well-being of those souls Christ Himself has chosen to be *alteri Christi* through the ministerial priesthood.

The unique bond between priest and "spiritual mother" is both tender and intensely powerful. How often I have heard priests speak affectionately of their spiritual mothers, grateful to them for nurturing the priestly vocation that had stirred within them as youngsters and faithfully nurturing that vocation with constant prayer, loving sacrifice, and wise counsel through their seminary days and beyond ordination. I have witnessed elderly priests who still gratefully recall the names of the religious sisters who taught them in elementary school and encouraged them to embrace their priestly vocation.

In the history of the Church, countless saintly women have ministered to priests in imitation of Mary. Out of all the Gospel passages that mention these women, the Gospel reading that the Church places on the feast of Our Lady of Mount Carmel is that of Mary accompanying Jesus at the foot of the Cross. It is a poignant reminder of our Carmelite charism to support priests by our prayers and sacrifices.

When St. Teresa of Ávila initiated her reform of the Carmelite order, it was for the purpose of praying for the needs of the Church and for priests. The Church in her time was being torn asunder by the Protestant Reformation, and St. Teresa was determined to do what she could to help the Church and priests. In *The Way of Perfection*, she counsels her spiritual daughters that they must "help our King" (Christ) by helping those He has chosen, "these servants of God who at the cost of so much toil, have fortified themselves with learning and virtuous living and have labored to help the Lord."[81]

In *The Story of a Soul*, St. Thérèse of the Child Jesus reiterated this vital mission of Carmel of praying for priests when telling her prioress of the trip to Rome she had made with her father and sisters before entering Carmel:

> If holy priests whom Jesus calls in the Gospel "the salt of the earth" show in their behavior that they have an extreme need of prayers, what can one say about the ones who are lukewarm? Didn't Jesus add, "But if the salt loses its saltiness, how can it be made salty again?" (Mt. 5:13)?
>
> Oh Mother! How beautiful is the vocation that has as its object to preserve the salt that is destined for souls! That vocation is Carmel's, since the only objective of our prayers and sacrifices is to be the apostle of the apostles, praying for them while they evangelize souls through their words and especially by their examples.[82]

Carmel's love of the priesthood was expressed by St. Teresa of the Andes, a young Chilean Carmelite, when she wrote:

> The goal the Carmelite proposes to herself is very great: to pray and sanctify herself for sinners and for priests. To become holy so that the divine sap

---

[81] St. Teresa of Ávila, *The Way of Perfection* (Sydney: E.J. Dwyer, 1988), 10.

[82] St. Thérèse of Lisieux, *Story of a Soul* (Brewster, MA: Paraclete Press, 2006), 134.

be communicated, by the union that exists between the faithful and all the members of the Church. She immolates herself on the cross, and her blood falls on sinners, imploring mercy and repentance for them. It falls on priests to sanctify them since on the cross she's intimately united with Jesus Christ. Her blood then is mixed with the divine.[83]

The Carmelite is the sister of the priest. Both offer a host of holocaust for the salvation of the world.... In a word, she sanctifies herself to sanctify her brothers.[84]

A young French Carmelite, Blessed Elizabeth of the Trinity, understood her apostolic work of prayer and sacrifice to be associated with the work of the priest and said, "The life of a priest — and that of a Carmelite — is an advent which prepares the way for the Incarnation in souls."[85]

To me, as a Carmelite Sister of the Most Sacred Heart of Los Angeles, praying for priests is as vital as breathing! To pray for my brothers "out in the trenches" is not only a great gift given to me, but also an immense responsibility that I do not take lightly. In fact, praying for priests is

---

[83] St. Teresa of the Andes, quoted in Michael Griffin, O.C.D., *Testimonies to Blessed Teresa of the Andes* (Washington, D.C.: Teresian Charism Press, 1995), 104-105.

[84] Ibid., 107.

[85] Blessed Elizabeth of the Trinity, quoted in Conrad de Meester, ed., *I Have Found God: Complete Works*, vol. 2 (Washington, D.C.: ICS Publications, 1995), 232-233.

of primary importance in our Congregation, and this is clearly expressed in our constitutions.

ᴊᵉ

SPIRITUAL EXERCISE
Lectio

1. "Whoever does the will of my Father in heaven is my brother, and sister, and mother" (Matt.12:50).

2. "Pray for one another, that you may be healed. The prayer of a righteous man has great power in its effects" (James 5:16).

3. "And he said to them, 'This kind cannot be driven out by anything but prayer and fasting'" (Mark 9:29).

Meditatio

Christ speaks to Venerable Conchita on the zeal of Mary for the sanctification of priests: "She was chosen from among all women so that the Incarnation of the Divine Word would be accomplished in her virginal womb. From that moment, the immaculate Virgin Mother did not cease to offer me up to him as the Victim who came from heaven to save the world, sacrificing her motherly heart to the divine will of the beloved Father. My sacrifice on the Cross and that accomplished in her heart were one sacrifice, which continued afterwards in the martyrdom of her solitude, in the martyrdom of her memories, the sufferings that she offered in union with me to the eternal Father."[86]

---

[86] Concepcion Cabrera de Armida, *Priests of Christ* (New York: St. Paul's, 2004), 282.

Spiritual Motherhood in Church History

Respond

1. Would you consider yourself to be a spiritual mother for priests? How?

2. What can you "take away" from reading about spiritual motherhood in the history of the Church?

3. When you pray for priests, what do you ask of God for them?

Prayer for Priests by St. Thérèse of Lisieux

O Jesus, Eternal Priest,
keep Your priests within
the shelter of Your Sacred Heart,
where none may touch them.
Keep unstained their anointed hands,
which daily touch Your Sacred Body.
Keep unsullied their lips, daily purpled
with Your Precious Blood.
Keep pure and unworldly their hearts,
sealed with the sublime mark
of Your priesthood.
Let Your holy love surround
them from the world's contagion.
Bless their labors with abundant fruit,
and may the souls to whom they minister
be their joy and consolation here
and their everlasting crown hereafter.
Mary, Queen of the Clergy, pray for us;
obtain for us numerous and holy priests.

4

_⚹_

The Holy Hour: An Encounter with Jesus

To contemplate the face of Christ, and
to contemplate it with Mary, is the "program"
which I have set before the Church
at the dawn of the third millennium, summoning
her to put out into the deep on the sea of history
with the enthusiasm of the new evangelization.[87]
—St. John Paul II

The initiative of prayer for priests calls for deepening our Eucharistic encounter with Jesus, rekindling Eucharistic amazement. We can then discover the secret of the Divine Presence as *the cure* for what ails humanity. St. Josemaría Escrivá wrote of this abiding presence:

Think of the human experience of two people who love each other, and yet are forced to part. They would like to stay together forever, but duty—in one form or another—forces

---

[87] *Ecclesia de Eucharistia*, no. 6.

them to separate. They are unable to fulfill their desire of remaining close to each other, so man's love—which, great as it may be, is limited—seeks a symbolic gesture. People who make their farewells exchange gifts or perhaps a photograph with a dedication so ardent that it seems almost enough to burn that piece of paper. They can do no more, because a creature's power is not as great as its desire. What we cannot do, our Lord is able to do. Jesus Christ, perfect God and perfect man, leaves us, not a symbol, but a reality. He himself stays with us. He will go to the Father, but he will also remain among men. He will leave us, not simply a gift that will make us remember him, not an image that becomes blurred over time, like a photograph that soon fades and has no meaning except for those who were contemporaries. Under the appearances of bread and wine, he is really present, with his body and blood, with his soul and divinity.[88]

In my travels, I have discovered among many Catholics a deep sense of privation, a longing in the human heart—a sense of absence and even estrangement from true communion with God. This is a paralyzing reality among believers. How can this be when Jesus is *always and truly present* in the Eucharist, on the altars and in the tabernacles of the world? Jesus hasn't abandoned us; He is perpetually present! Often we claim to be looking for God, but our back is turned to Him as we look to people and places where God is not found. We have to turn around to look at Jesus—face-to-face in the Eucharist—to make sense of the madness of the world all around us.

[88] Josemaría Escrivá de Balaguer, *Christ Is Passing By* (Chicago: Scepter Press, 1990), 121-122.

The Holy Hour: An Encounter with Jesus

There is a *great thirst* among God's people, but the thirst of Jesus is far greater. The Heart of the Eternal High Priest is not fickle like the human heart. The Church's initiatives, including the crusade of prayer for priests, will be fruitful only if we fall in love with Jesus in the Eucharist. The Eucharist is the deepest, most life-changing encounter with Jesus the High Priest!

The name *Jesus the Eternal High Priest* is intimately related to *His hour* when in Gethsemane Jesus prayed to the Father and to His perfect sacrifice on the altar of the Cross. Scripture describes Jesus as a priest in this way:

> Since then we have a great high priest who has passed through the heavens, Jesus, the Son of God, let us hold fast our confession. For we have not a high priest who is unable to sympathize with our weaknesses, but one who in every respect has been tempted as we are, yet without sinning. Let us then with confidence draw near to the throne of grace, that we may receive mercy and find grace to help in time of need. (Heb. 4:14-16)

The Lord "sympathizes with our weaknesses"; therefore, let us have confidence in Him. The Eternal High Priest is a "victim offering" to God the Father for the ransom of humanity. Each ministerial priest becomes a victim offering also.

Archbishop Fulton Sheen eloquently writes about this to his brother priests:

> That moment when the priest lifts up the Host and the Chalice, he is at his best. A bride and groom are at their peak of loveliness and lovability at the moment of marriage. Love is said to be blind because it sees no faults in the beloved. God's love becomes blind at this moment. He

sees us through "the rose-colored glasses" of his Son. Never again will we appear as priestly, as victimal, as deserving of salvation, as we are when the Father sees us through "the rose-colored glasses" of the Body and Blood of his Son as we lift Host and Chalice to heaven. During this holy action, we priests become holy (Exodus 39:29). But we are also victims. We do not just *offer* Mass; we are also *offered*.[89]

If we take time to ponder these sublime truths of our Faith, we are struck with awe at the gift of God. He loved us into being, ransomed us from sin and death by laying down His life so that we can live forever, and then perpetuates Himself in the ministerial priesthood so that we can encounter the living Jesus made present by His priests.

The letter to the Hebrews says, "Since then we have a great high priest who has passed through the heavens, Jesus, the Son of God, let us hold fast our confession." What does it mean to hold fast our confession? We confess that Jesus is Lord; we confess our faith in and love for Christ. We bear witness by our life and our good works. How can our confession of faith and love for Jesus be convincing if we are not encountering him? The Holy Hour is one way to encounter Jesus personally.

In its 2012 booklet, the Congregation for the Clergy included a suggested protocol for *public or parish* observance of a Holy Hour.[90] In many areas of the world, Eucharistic adoration is not readily available to the faithful. Therefore, I offer this chapter inviting everyone to pray (as often as possible) a *private* Holy

---

[89] Fulton Sheen, *Those Mysterious Priests* (Staten Island, NY: Alba House, 2005), 159-160, emphasis added.

[90] *Eucharistic Adoration for the Sanctification of Priests and Spiritual Maternity*, 43-47.

The Holy Hour: An Encounter with Jesus

Hour before the tabernacle in their church to encounter Jesus, to deepen their personal relationship with Him, and to participate in the mission of interceding for priests and vocations.

Fr. Raniero Cantalamessa illustrates how Eucharistic adoration can be an individual or group experience:

> Eucharistic adoration may be personal or communal; in fact, it expresses the full force of what it signifies when an assembly is before the Blessed Sacrament, singing, praising, or simply kneeling. This invitatory psalm, with which the Liturgy of the Hours opens every day, aptly expresses the shared character of adoration: "O come, let us worship and bow down, let us kneel before the Lord, our Maker!" (Psalm 95:6).[91]

The Holy Hour is meant to be an encounter with the living Jesus. It is an exercise of love, not a project to be accomplished. One hour with the Divine Sacrament will improve the quality of the remaining twenty-three. Communing with the Divine Lover of our soul becomes irresistible joy, not labor. The words of Bl. Teresa of Calcutta inspire us: "When you look at the Crucifix, you understand how much Jesus loved you then. When you look at the Sacred Host you understand how much Jesus loves you now."[92] Twenty-five years ago, my priest spiritual director encouraged me to stay after daily Mass to pray a Holy Hour. He

[91] Raniero Cantalamessa, *This Is My Body: Eucharistic Reflections Inspired by Adoro Te Devote and Ave Verum* (Boston: Pauline Books and Media, 2005), 25.

[92] Quoted in *At the Altar of the World: The Pontificate of Pope John Paul II through the Lens of L'Osservatore Romano and the Words of Ecclesia de Eucharistia* (Washington, D.C.: Pope John Paul II Cultural Center, 2003), 170.

explained that the Mass is the Church's prayer; and the Holy Hour would be my personal time with the Lord. A daily Holy Hour has been transformative for me.

Some may be wondering if there is a formula the Church recommends for making a Holy Hour. In the guidance I've received from my spiritual directors over the years, and in reflecting on my own experience with Eucharistic adoration, I humbly submit to you the following recommendations:

- Come into Jesus's presence with expectant faith and humility.

- Greet Jesus with honor, praise, and gratitude.

- Recollect yourself by reading a psalm or another Scripture passage or praying the holy Rosary.

- Offer prayers of petition (intercessory prayer).

- Allow ample time to listen in silence.

- Rest in the silent presence of Jesus.

- Receive His love and inspiration.

- Encounter Jesus in an intimate friendship.

If you fall asleep, think of how a medical surgeon puts his patient under anesthesia so he can operate on him while he is unconscious. Jesus can operate on your soul in a similar manner while you rest or even sleep! Do not be anxious about the right or wrong formula or prayers, but show reverence and docility to the way that Jesus moves your heart. Cultivate a listening heart. Jesus is pleased to have your company!

Let us also consider the wisdom of Archbishop Sheen as he addresses priests regarding how to make a Holy Hour. This advice can easily apply to laypeople as well:

The Holy Hour: An Encounter with Jesus

No rules—just spend a continuous hour before the Blessed Sacrament. If however, a part of the hour were made before Mass and the rest of it after Mass, that would still be continuous....

I remember having two hours between trains in Paris. I went to the Church of St. Roch to make my Holy Hour. There are not ten days a year when I can sleep in the daytime. This was one. I was so tired, I sat down at 2:00 p.m.—too tired to kneel, and went to sleep. I slept perfectly until 3:00 p.m. I said to the Good Lord: "Did I make a Holy Hour?" The answer came back: "Yes! That's the way the Apostles made their first one." The best time to make it is in the morning, early, before the day sets traps for us.[93]

Occasionally, if we are sleepy during our Holy Hours, we should not lose our peace of soul. After all, does a loving parent get upset when his little child falls asleep in his arms? God is our loving parent. But it's also true that parents enjoy seeing their children when they're alert!

Encountering Jesus through Intercessory Prayer

When we pray for priests and vocations, or ask anything on behalf of another, we petition God the Father through the intercession of the Eternal High Priest. As I grew closer to Jesus through a deepening prayer life, I became attuned to the intentions of His priestly Heart.

Prayer is always powerful, but intercessory prayer is uniquely aligned to the heart of the Eternal High Priest, who now lives at the right hand of the Father, interceding for the human family.

[93] *Those Mysterious Priests*, 193.

Praying for Priests

Prayer changes situations, and it transforms human hearts. Prayer not only draws graces on the priest or the person for whom we are praying; it also draws grace into the hearts of us pray-*ers* who offer petitions to God in faith, with love and hope.

Prayer is meant to be a *personal encounter* with Jesus. The splendors of the Eucharist and the glories of the Eternal High Priest are as lofty as the heavens and as infinite as divine love. We are invited to rediscover the sublime beauty of the love of Jesus that remains with us in the Sacred Host. We need to rediscover the gift of God in the Eucharist to rediscover the gift of the priest, who makes Jesus present there.

Encountering Jesus through Eucharistic Amazement

In 2003, Pope John Paul II laid out a plan for rekindling Eucharistic amazement. Less than five years later, Cláudio Cardinal Hummes, then prefect for the Congregation for the Clergy, invoked Mary in a letter to bishops around the world, inviting them to further Pope John Paul II's program via Eucharistic adoration:

> By becoming her children, we learn the true meaning of life in Christ. Thereby—and precisely because of the role of the Most Blessed Virgin in salvation history—we intend to entrust in a very particular way all priests to Mary, the Mother of the Eternal High Priest, bringing about in the Church *a movement of prayer, placing 24-hour Eucharistic adoration at the center, so that prayers of adoration, thanksgiving and praise, petition and reparation will be raised to God, incessantly and from every corner of the earth, with the primary intention of awakening a sufficient number of holy vocations to the priestly state, while at the same time spiritually and maternally uniting—at the level*

of the Mystical Body—all those who have already been on-tologically conformed to the one Eternal High Priest through the ministerial priesthood. This movement will offer better service to Christ and his brothers—those who are both "inside" the Church and "at the forefront" of the Church, standing in Christ's stead and representing him, as head, shepherd and spouse of the Church.[94]

The invitation by the Congregation suggests two things that will "offer better service to Christ and his brothers": entrustment to Mary and Eucharistic adoration. The word *better* indicates that we need to do more in this area because there is an increasing need for interior renewal of priests for growth in sanctification. Interior renewal is closely connected with inner healing. We recognize the urgent need for healing in the Church.

Fr. Cantalamessa writes about the healing power of "Eucharistic contemplation":

Eucharistic contemplation also has an extraordinary power of healing. In the desert God ordered Moses to raise a bronze serpent on a pole. All those who were bitten by poisonous snakes and then looked at the bronze serpent were healed (cf. Numbers 21:4-9). Jesus applied the mysterious symbol of the bronze serpent to himself (John 3:14). What we should do, then, when afflicted by the venomous bites of pride, sensuality, and all the other illnesses of the soul is not to get lost in vain considerations or seek excuses, but to run before the Most Blessed Sacrament, to look at the Host and let healing

---

[94] Cláudio Cardinal Hummes, Letter to Bishops, December 8, 2007, emphasis added.

pass through the same organ through which evil so often passes: our eyes.

The only thing the Holy Spirit asks of us is that we give him our time, even if at the beginning it might seem like lost time. I will never forget the lesson that was given to me one day in this regard. I said to God, "Lord, give me fervor and I will give you all the time you desire in prayer." I found the answer in my heart: "Raniero, give me your time and I will give you all the fervor you want in prayer."[95]

Our eyes are meant to behold what is holy, good, true, and beautiful. Unfortunately, our eyes are bombarded by worldly things that are unholy and ugly. Gazing upon the face of Jesus and contemplating His beauty, purity, and goodness is the healing balm we need to be renewed.

Jesus awaits us in every tabernacle of the world where the glow of the sanctuary lamp invites us to come and *be* with the One who has proven His love for us. His life, death, and Resurrection are proofs of His love. Further proof of the extravagance of His love for humanity are the sacraments, of which the Eucharist is the crown jewel.

Although we may have good intentions, we often fail to pray or visit Jesus in the Blessed Sacrament because our daily lives are too busy. It is countercultural to come apart simply to *be* with the Lord. Learning how to *rest in God* is a gift of prayer called *contemplation*.[96] Contemplative prayer leads to a deep, abiding

---

[95] *This Is My Body*, 33.

[96] *Contemplation* derives from the Latin word *contemplatio*, which means "rest." In contemplative prayer, we rest in God's love and let grace work in us.

encounter with God. Fr. Cantalamessa writes, "Contemplation is an eminently personal activity; it calls for silence and requires that one be isolated from everything and everyone to concentrate on the object contemplated and to be lost in it."[97]

Through the gift of faith, we discover the *Divine Somebody* whose love is incomprehensible, extravagant, healing, and infinitely perfect. No one can encounter Jesus and remain the same, because an experience of divine love changes everything. An authentic encounter with Jesus in the silence of prayer leads to conversion of heart. Constancy in prayer leads to perpetual conversion; absent prayer, conversion will cease. Through an authentic encounter with Jesus, we change from within—we turn toward God and away from what is not of God. The process of encounter and conversion leads to engagement with Jesus in a deep personal relationship of mutual love and friendship.

There is a progression:

+ *Encounter* with Jesus: personal experience in silence / contemplation;

+ *Conversion* of heart: movement toward God and away from what is not of God;

+ *Engagement* with Jesus in a relationship of love that leads to service.

Here, I am reminded of the famous words of St. Mother Teresa of Calcutta:

> *The fruit of silence is prayer.*
> *The fruit of prayer is faith.*
> *The fruit of faith is love.*

---

[97] *This Is My Body*, 25.

Praying for Priests

The fruit of love is service.
The fruit of service is peace.[98]

Jesus is always present for us on the altars of His Church, in the tabernacles of the world. He awaits us there, but He also initiates an encounter with us. What's more, He also goes out after us—He pursues us to the ends of the earth, seeking after the human family like the Good Shepherd who left the ninety-nine sheep to search for the one lost lamb. No matter where we may run or hide, He is there—inviting us to an encounter of love. This is the most touching thing to me. It is not that we have loved Him but that He has loved us first (cf. 1 John 4:10).

Jesus is the stupendous Divine Lover who always does amazing things in pursuit of His people. During my daily Holy Hour, I often gaze at the hidden God in the Sacred Host in awe of the humility of Jesus, who condescends to become so little and vulnerable to His creatures. I beg my Lord to make me humble, to crucify my pride, which hides itself in so many clever ways unknown to me. What a relief it is for me to come before Jesus without pretense. It is refreshing to be utterly transparent before God. Many times He has allowed me to see myself in the light of truth, and I repeat the words of Peter, "Depart from me, Lord, for I am a sinner" (cf. Luke 5:8). Then I am filled with blessed assuredness of divine mercy that absorbs my forgiven sins. Jesus is merciful even in His discipline of the soul. He draws us to His Sacred Heart, where the fire of divine love burns away the dross

---

[98] Quoted in Fr. Brian Kolodiejchuk, M.C., *Where There Is Love, There Is God: A Path to Closer Union with God and Greater Love for Others* (New York: Image, 2012), 16.

of our fallen nature. Then slowly but surely we are purified in the embers of divine love.

Jesus the Eternal High Priest remains with us so that we may have abundant life on earth and eternal life in heaven. God knows how desperate we are to encounter him. He knows that without the encounter of divine love, we languish amid many counterfeit loves.

Recall the encounter between Jesus and Zacchaeus (Luke 19:1-10). Zacchaeus, a crooked tax collector, short in stature, climbed a tree so that he could see Jesus passing by. He was probably just curious. But Jesus noticed him and called him by name to come down from the tree because He wanted to go to his house. Jesus knew Zacchaeus needed to encounter the truth that would set him free. Because of that merciful encounter with Jesus, salvation came to the house of Zacchaeus, a sinner. Jesus initiated the encounter with Zacchaeus that day. In our day, Jesus continues to initiate the encounter because He is present and waiting in every tabernacle of the world. Jesus has already shown up; He waits for us to show up too.

When we come to worship and adore Jesus in the Blessed Sacrament, we must come as we are—sinners in need of a Savior. We may not feel the experience emotionally, but we will discover the existence of divine love animating us through life in moments of joy and sorrow, in consolation and desolation.

Offering a Holy Hour for Priests

When I offer a Holy Hour for priests, I invoke the Holy Spirit to lead me in praying for the priest in greatest need of help. I reflect on the encounter between Jesus and Bartimaeus (Mark 10:46-52), in which Jesus asks, "What do you want me to do for you?" Bartimaeus replies, "I want to see." In my time with Jesus, I want to see how to help a priest in need of prayer.

Praying for Priests

I believe that Jesus wants to lead us in prayer, for He takes no delight in spiritual blindness or deadness. He desires for us to come into the light of the Holy of Holies so that we might pray to the Father, commune with heaven, and receive strength and wisdom for the journey.

I read a book entitled *To My Priests*, which records the Lord's words to Ven. Conchita. The words she received more than eighty years ago are relevant still:

> I want to rebuild the sunken hearts of many of my priests; I want to wake up their slumbering souls; I want to move the loving fibers in the very depths of priestly hearts that they might respond to my longing to perfect them in unity; I want my protests to penetrate their sentiments sickened by contact with a world that has distanced them from me.
>
> I want to bring them into my arms, press them to my heart, and impart fire, light, love, life! I confide to you that my heart full of tenderness and charity deeply desires all of this.
>
> I promise that this heavenly impulse for my priests will not remain unfulfilled; it will make itself felt at a future time throughout the world.[99]

On one occasion, during a time of adoration following Holy Thursday Mass, Jesus spoke in the silence of my heart. I wrote in my private prayer journal:

> I saw them all that night in the Upper Room—each unique brother of mine who would share the cup of royalty and

---

[99] A *Mis Sacerdotes*, 306-307, 308 (text translated by John Nahrgang).

become marked with the seal of sacramental priesthood. I saw their goodness, intent on doing as I told them. They listened intently to the Master, and I loved them as I love myself. I knew them and loved them with the most unfathomable divine charity! That night, the first Twelve were with me physically, but all men who would follow their footsteps were in my mind's eye and in my heart. I knew their future. I saw a brotherhood of heroic faith, hope, and love that would catch souls for the Kingdom. I knew also the future Judases—the few unfaithful brothers among all the faithful. I saw the troubles that would plague my priesthood down through the ages. I saw all those who would betray me and wound the Bride, the Church. I saw the many who would remain always faithful to me. I considered all human weakness and chose to perpetuate myself through these chosen men. I know my royal priesthood, the brothers of my heart—I know them and love them with all my divine love!

In light of sharing the words above, I propose some thoughts from a great theologian regarding the interior life: how we hear and listen to God's voice. Fr. Reginald Garrigou-Lagrange, O.P., wrote the spiritual classic *The Three Stages of the Interior Life*. This is one of the first books I read in my mid-thirties, when I was resuming a serious prayer life. It was through this priest's teachings that I felt comfortable opening my heart to interior conversation with God in the normal progression of the interior life. Fr. Garrigou-Lagrange teaches:

> The interior life thus becomes more and more a conversation with God, in which man gradually frees himself from egoism, self-love, sensuality, and pride, in which, by frequent prayer, he asks the Lord for the ever-new graces

he needs. His interior conversation changes so much that St. Paul can say, "Our conversation is in Heaven." St. Thomas often insisted on this point.

Therefore, the interior life is in a soul that is in the state of grace, especially in a life of humility, abnegation, faith, hope and charity with the peace given by the progressive subordination of our feelings and wishes to love God, who will be the object of our beatitude.

Hence, to have an interior life, an exceedingly active exterior apostolate does not suffice, nor does great theological knowledge; nor is the latter necessary. A generous beginner, who already has a genuine spirit of abnegation and prayer, already possesses a true interior life, which ought to continue developing.

Prayer takes the form of petition, of adoration, and thanksgiving; it is always an elevation of the soul toward God. And God answers by recalling to our minds what has been said to us in the Gospel, and what is useful for the sanctification of the present moment. Did not Christ say, "But the Paraclete, the Holy Spirit, whom the Father will send in my name, he will teach you all things and bring all things to your mind whatsoever I shall have said to you" (John 14:26)?[100]

We Wish to See Jesus

Pope John Paul II once reflected upon these words from the Gospel: "We wish to see Jesus" (John 12:21).

---

[100] Fr. Reginald Garrigou-Lagrange, O.P., *The Three Ages of the Interior Life*, vol. 1 (Rockford, IL: TAN Books, 1989), 46.

The Holy Hour: An Encounter with Jesus

This request, addressed to the Apostle Philip by some Greeks who had made a pilgrimage to Jerusalem for the Passover, echoes spiritually in our ears. Like those pilgrims of two thousand years ago, the men and women of our own day—often unconsciously—ask believers not only to *speak* of Christ, but in a certain sense to *show* him to them. And the Church's task is to reflect the light of Christ in every historical period, and to make his face shine before generations. Our witness, however, would be hopelessly inadequate if we ourselves had not first *contemplated his face*.[101]

Recall the biblical encounters of Peter with the Eternal High Priest at the various stages of his journey— the initial *yes* of Peter to follow Jesus, his eventual *denial* of Jesus, and then the *encounters* with Jesus, first on the day of His Resurrection, then on the shore of Galilee when the risen Lord reinstated Peter by asking him three times if he loved Him, received three yeses, and then asked him to feed his sheep (John 21:15-17).

These Petrine encounters reveal God's mercy for an ordinary chosen man upon whom He built His Church. Peter is changed incrementally, as most of us are. His encounters with Christ strengthened him on the path to his own crucifixion for the sake of love. Peter said yes quickly, then fell to temptation quickly, but picked himself up and began again to fulfill his unique mission as the first Vicar of Christ.

We should not deprive ourselves of a daily encounter with Jesus. Furthermore, through the Church, He invites us now to

---

[101] John Paul II, *Novo Millennio Ineunte*, no. 16.

bring our intercessory prayer to the tabernacle to pray for the sanctification of priests and for vocations.

Why do we need to carry all priests to the tabernacle? Ven. Archbishop Sheen reveals the reason:

> Supplication, mediation and pleading have always been heard by God. Wrath would have been visited on the Jewish people had not Moses interceded (Exodus 32:9-14, Deuteronomy 9:18, 20, 25-28). Job interceded for the three counseling specialists who gave him wrong answers (Job 42:8-10). Even in marriage: "For the heathen husband now belongs to God through his Christian wife and the heathen wife through her Christian husband" (1 Corinthians 7:14). There is no reason to suppose that this would not apply to cities or nations if there were sufficiently holy priests, as Sodom and Gomorrah would have been saved for ten just men.
>
> In medicine, when a patient is suffering from anemia, blood will be transferred from a healthy person to cure the sick of that condition. Skin is grafted from the back to the face to repair a burn. If blood can be transfused and skin grafted, then prayers and sacrifices can be transmitted to the sick members of the Mystical Body of Christ. The motivation for a Holy Hour is reparation. We pray for those who do not pray, we make acts of faith in the Real Presence for those who lack or who have lost the faith. In a word, we are their victims, like Christ, innocent but one with their guilt in the progressive redemption of mankind. The Holy Hour in our modern rat race is necessary for authentic prayer.[102]

---

[102] *Those Mysterious Priests*, 187.

The Holy Hour: An Encounter with Jesus

Jesus Invites Us to Carry Priests to Adoration

Recorded in the prayer journal of an anonymous Benedictine monk, Jesus reveals, "I have called you to this life of adoration to make up for the coldness and indifference of so many priests who, while living close to My sacramental presence, rarely if ever come before My Face and approach My Eucharistic Heart. This is one of My greatest sorrows; that the men whom I have chosen and set apart to be My friends and My priests show so little interest in remaining in My company, in listening to what I have to say to them, and in pouring out their hearts to Me. I wait for them. I look for their arrival."[103]

⁘

SPIRITUAL EXERCISE

Lectio

1. Wrath would have been visited on the Jewish people had not Moses interceded (Exod. 32:9-14, Deut. 9:18, 20, 25-28).

2. "We wish to see Jesus" (John 12:21).

3. "Let us then with confidence draw near to the throne of grace, that we may receive mercy and find grace to help in time of need" (Heb. 4:16).

Meditatio

St. John Vianney: "When you enter the church and take holy water, and when you raise your hand to your forehead to make the sign of the cross, look at the tabernacle. At the

---

[103] *In Sinu Jesu*, 99.

same time our Lord Jesus Christ opens it to bless you, and says to you, 'Come to me, all you that are weary and sink under your burden, and I will refresh you.' Thanks be to you, O Jesus, for this word from your kind heart. Oh? How sweet it is to hear it in the midst of life's dreariness and confusion! It illumines and rekindles my soul like a ray of sunlight."[104]

Respond

1. At Mass or Adoration, how have you encountered Jesus in the Eucharist?

2. Recall a time or incident when you realized the power of intercessory prayer.

3. Is there some adjustment to your schedule that could be made to allow for frequent reception of the Eucharist at Mass, or time in Adoration?

Prayer

Jesus, Eternal High Priest,
graciously draw us into an abiding
encounter of divine love through
Your Eucharistic Presence.
In the glow of the sanctuary lamp,
let us meet You in expectant faith.
In silent contemplation, let us
receive Your holy instruction.

---

[104] St. John Vianney, *The Cure of Ars and the Holy Eucharist* (Long Prairie, MN: Neumann Press, 2000), 115.

The Holy Hour: An Encounter with Jesus

*Attract us in prayer and give us
an abiding desire to live in accord
with Your Eucharistic Heart.*

*Convert our hearts,
heal our wounds, and empower
us to bear witness to others,
that we might fulfill this
mission of prayer for priests
for the salvation of souls.*

5

⚜

The Holy Rosary: A School of Prayer

The Rosary, reclaimed in its full meaning,
goes to the very heart of Christian life;
it offers a familiar yet fruitful spiritual and
educational opportunity for personal contemplation,
the formation of the People of God,
and the new evangelization.[105]
—St. John Paul II

Pope John Paul II in his 2004 apostolic letter for the Year of the
Eucharist, wrote about the Rosary as an aid to contemplation:

Let us deepen through adoration our personal and commu-
nal contemplation, drawing upon aids to prayer inspired by
the word of God and the experience of so many mystics,
old and new. The Rosary itself, when it is profoundly understood in the biblical and Christocentric form ... will
prove a particularly fitting introduction to Eucharistic

[105] *Rosarium Virginis Mariae*, no. 3.

contemplation, contemplation carried out with Mary as our companion and guide.[106]

The Rosary is principally composed of the prayer of Christ, the *Our Father*, and the Angelic Salutation, the *Hail Mary*. In his 2002 apostolic letter *Rosarium Virginis Mariae* (*On the Most Holy Rosary*), Pope John Paul II develops this dynamic further:

> The Rosary of the Virgin Mary, which gradually took form in the second millennium under the guidance of the Spirit of God, is a prayer loved by countless saints and encouraged by the Magisterium. Simple yet profound, it still remains, at the dawn of this third millennium, a prayer of great significance destined to bring forth a harvest of holiness. It blends easily into the spiritual journey of the Christian life, which, after two thousand years, has lost none of the freshness of its beginning and feels drawn by the Spirit of God to "set out into the deep" (*duc in altum!*) in order once more to proclaim, and even cry out, before the world that Jesus Christ is Lord and Savior, "the way, and the truth and the life" (Jn 14:6), "the goal of human history and the point on which the desires of history and civilization turn."

The Rosary, though clearly Marian in character, is at heart a Christocentric prayer. In the sobriety of its elements, it has all the *depth of the Gospel message in its entirety*, of which it can be said to be a compendium. It is an echo of the prayer of Mary, her perennial *Magnificat* for the work of redemptive Incarnation, which began in her virginal womb. With the Rosary, the Christian people *sits at the school of Mary* and is led to contemplate the beauty of the face of Christ and to experience the depths of his love. Through the Rosary, the faithful receive abundant grace, as though from the very hands of the Mother of the Redeemer.[107]

Pope John Paul II was often seen and pictured with a rosary in his hand. I wonder how many thousands of rosaries he gave to the faithful who came to his papal audiences. The Polish pope spoke from the heart about the impact of the Rosary on him and on his pontificate:

I myself have often encouraged the frequent recitation of the Rosary. From my youthful years this prayer has held an important place in my spiritual life. I was powerfully reminded of this during my recent visit to Poland, and in particular at the Shrine of Kalwaria. The Rosary has accompanied me in moments of joy and in moments of difficulty. To it I have entrusted any number of concerns; in it I have always found comfort. Twenty-four years ago, 29 October 1978, scarcely two weeks after my election to the See of Peter, I frankly admitted: "The Rosary is my favorite prayer. A marvelous prayer! Marvelous in its simplicity and its depth!... Against the background of the words *Ave Maria* the principal events of the life of Jesus Christ pass before the eyes of the soul. They take shape in the complete series of the joyful, sorrowful, and glorious mysteries, and they put us in living communion with Jesus through—we might say—the heart of his Mother. At the same time our

---

[107] *Rosarium Virginis Mariae*, no. 1.

hearts can embrace in the decades of the Rosary all the events that make up the lives of individuals, families, nations, the Church, and all mankind; our personal concerns and those of our neighbor, especially those who are closest to us, who are dearest to us. Thus the simple prayers of the Rosary mark the rhythm of human life."

... How many graces have I received in these from the Blessed Virgin through the Rosary: *Magnificat anima mea Dominum!* I wish to lift up my thanks to the Lord in the words of his Most Holy Mother, under whose protection I have placed my Petrine ministry: *Totus Tuus!*[108]

The Rosary Is a Weapon of Prayer

The Rosary is a *contemplative* prayer and an *intercessory* prayer. It is also a *weapon* against the evil one. In 1951, Pius XII wrote in the encyclical *Ingruentium Malorum*, "We do not hesitate to again affirm publicly the great hope that we put in the Rosary to heal the evils that afflict our time. Not with force, not with arms, not with human power, but with divine help obtained by means of this prayer, the Church, strong like David with his sling, will be able to confront the infernal enemy unafraid."

In Pope John Paul II's apostolic letter *Rosarium Virginis Mariae*, he writes, "The Church has always attributed a particular efficacy to this prayer, entrusting to the Rosary, to its choral recitation, to its constant practice, the most difficult problems. At times when Christianity itself was threatened, its deliverance was attributed to the power of this prayer, and Our Lady of the Rosary was acclaimed as the one whose intercession brought salvation" (no. 39).

---

[108] *Rosarium Virginis Mariae*, no. 2.

The Holy Rosary: A School of Prayer

I have witnessed this as part of a team helping priests in official rites of exorcism. The devil and his legions are real, and they detest Mary and her holy Rosary! Once, during intense deliverance prayers by our priest leader, the demon screamed through the mouth of the poor victim, "Stop saying those beads! Those beads burn me!" Unbeknownst to the victim, her mother was in an upstairs room praying continuous Rosaries for her daughter. In my experience of assisting at exorcisms, the Rosary has been continuously prayed, either silently or aloud. The *Catechism* asserts that prayer is a battle and that man's entire life is a battle against the evil one (nos. 409, 2725). God made a provision for this by equipping the Church with an arsenal of spiritual power (the sacraments and sacramentals) to make us victorious over evil. The Rosary is one of the primary weapons of prayer. I observed that demons react most powerfully against the words of Scripture and anything having to do with Mary. The Rosary is both a Marian prayer and a scriptural prayer, so it is a weapon that does tremendous damage to the demonic world.

The Scriptural Rosary:
A Compendium of the Gospel

In *Rosarium Virginis Mariae*, John Paul II referred to the Rosary as a "compendium of the Gospel" and added the five Luminous Mysteries to the original fifteen mysteries of the Rosary:

> For the Rosary to become more fully a "compendium of the Gospel," it is fitting to add, following reflection on the Incarnation and the hidden life of Christ (*the joyful mysteries*) and before focusing on the sufferings of his Passion (*the sorrowful mysteries*) and triumph of his Resurrection (*the glorious mysteries*), a meditation on certain particularly

significant moments in his public ministry (*the mysteries of light*). This addition of these new mysteries, without prejudice to any essential aspect of the prayer's traditional format, is meant to give it fresh life and to enkindle renewed interest in the Rosary's place within Christian spirituality as a true doorway to the depths of the Heart of Christ, ocean of joy and light, of suffering and of glory.[109]

To contemplate the life of Christ with Mary is, for many Catholics, *the secret to deeper intimacy* with the Lord. Perhaps its miraculous effects should not surprise us, since it is based on the living Word of God, which is always effective, alive, and fruitful!

The Rosary Contains Mary's Memories

Pope John Paul II wrote that Mary remembers Christ in a "biblical sense," meaning that the memories do not only belong to history but *"they are also part of the 'today' of salvation."*[110] In a sense, remembering *makes salvation history present* with its gift of grace. Remembering Jesus and what He has done for us (the Paschal mystery) is necessary for gratitude and a thriving faith.

This is also true of our personal history. For example, our extended family joined hands in prayer around our dinner table one recent Thanksgiving. Each person shared a reason for being grateful. After dinner, my eighty-year-old parents handed each of their five children an envelope containing many old photos taken of us as we were growing up in the fifties, sixties, and seventies. We spent hours together remembering occasions from our

---

[109] *Rosarium Virginis Mariae*, no. 19.
[110] Ibid., no. 13.

lives over the past fifty years. It was joyous to recall our family history and marvel at the passage of time and how we had grown! In recalling these episodes from our family life, our hearts were filled with awe and gratitude. And some moments in the pictures we not only remembered but somehow relived.

Mary remembers Christ and the history of salvation better than anyone else, since she accompanied her Son on His earthly pilgrimage. In *Rosarium Virginis Mariae*, Pope John Paul II writes about Mary's memories:

> Mary lived with her eyes fixed on Christ, treasuring his every word: "She kept all these things, pondering them in her heart" (Luke 2:19; cf. 2:51). The memories of Jesus, impressed upon her heart, were always with her, leading her to reflect on the various moments of her life at her Son's side. In a way those memories were to be the "rosary" which she recited uninterruptedly through her earthly life.
>
> Even now, amid the joyful songs of the heavenly Jerusalem, the reasons for her thanksgiving and praise remain unchanged. They inspire her maternal concern for the pilgrim Church, in which she continues to relate her personal account of the Gospel. *Mary constantly sets before the faithful the "mysteries" of her Son*, with the desire that the contemplation of those mysteries will release all their saving power. In the recitation of the Rosary, the Christian community enters into contact with the memories and the contemplative gaze of Mary.[111]

When we pray Mary's Rosary, we walk with her, but she points us to Jesus. She teaches us to keep the memory of Christ

[111] Ibid., no. 11.

alive within our hearts. Mary accompanied the Eternal High Priest in a way no other person did. That is why the Church looks to the Mother of the Eternal High Priest to help us understand the dignity and vocation of all priests so that we can grow to love them as she does, even to love them *with her maternal heart*. The praying of the Rosary helps us to open ourselves so that Mary can teach us to intercede for priests and vocations. Her maternal charity for priests can be *infused* into our hearts as we ponder the mysteries of Christ's life. She will help us fall in love with Jesus and His priests. Mary also keeps us mindful of the invaluable gift that the priest gives to the Church, the Eucharist.

I pray the Rosary *for* priests and seminarians, but I also pray the Rosary *with* priests and seminarians, in person and over the phone. When I pray the Rosary with priests, it is edifying to see the myriad of intentions they bring to prayer. The needs and concerns of all their parishioners, brother priests and bishops, their families, the Church, and the world are carried in their priestly hearts. While praying the Rosary, they offer these intentions to the Heart of Mary with trust in her maternal mediation. The priests I know truly inspire me to live Catholicism with ardent gratitude and joy. They are my heroes!

Praying the Scriptural Rosary for Priests

The following chapters of this book contain scriptural Rosaries for priests, vocations, and reparation. They draw from Holy Scripture and from two important documents written by Pope John Paul II: *Pastores Dabo Vobis* and *Salvifici Dolores*.

I invite you to become a vessel of prayer for priests through the intercessory prayer of the Rosary.

The Holy Rosary: A School of Prayer

SPIRITUAL EXERCISE

Lectio

1. "Behold, I stand at the door and knock; if any one hears my voice and opens the door, I will come in to him and eat with him, and he with me" (Rev. 3:20).

2. "And they devoted themselves to the apostles' teaching and fellowship, to the breaking of bread and the prayers" (Acts 2:42).

3. "After this Jesus, knowing that all was now finished, said, 'I thirst'" (John 19:28).

Meditatio

"Mary's mission is to snatch souls from Satan so that she might make of God's enemies who are ready to fall into hell, his friends, his well-beloved children, who will praise him eternally in heaven. The glory of God and his love for his poor creatures are therefore also at stake. But since she has need of us, Mary cannot achieve these results without our help. Let us imagine if we can, how close to her heart the glory of the Most Blessed Trinity and the love of the heavenly Father for his children on earth must be. We might then grasp how much she must desire this help."[112]

---

[112] Fr. Emile Neubert, SM, *Mary's Apostolic Mission and Ours* (New Bedford, MA: Academy of the Immaculate, 2011), 288-289.

Respond

1. Do you believe that praying the Rosary is a school of prayer for you? How?

2. How would you describe your relationship with Mother Mary?

3. Have you experienced the Rosary as a powerful spiritual weapon?

Prayer

Mary, Queen of the Holy Rosary,
Mother of Priests and of the Church,
teach us to pray. Your Immaculate Heart is
a school of prayer. We place ourselves there
as your pupils. Pray that the Holy Spirit
will fill us with ardor for Jesus Christ
and zeal for the salvation of souls.
Write on our hearts God's Word
so that we may faithfully live out
the joyful, sorrowful, glorious and
luminous mysteries of our journey. Amen.

Part 2

❧

Rosary Reflections and Prayers

How to Pray the Scriptural Rosaries
in this Book

Sign of the Cross
Apostles' Creed
Our Father
Hail Mary (three times, for the
virtues of faith, hope, and charity)
Glory Be
Fátima Prayer

Announce the first mystery.
Read the Scripture passage,
the reflection, and the petition.
Our Father
Hail Mary (ten times while meditating
on the mystery for this decade)
Glory Be
Fátima Prayer
(Continue with the
remaining four mysteries.)

Hail, Holy Queen
Rosary Prayer

✤

Prayers of the Rosary

Sign of the Cross

In the name of the Father, and of the Son, and of the
Holy Spirit. Amen.

Apostles' Creed

I believe in God, the Father almighty, Creator of Heaven
and earth, and in Jesus Christ, His only Son, our Lord,
who was conceived by the Holy Spirit, born of the Virgin
Mary, suffered under Pontius Pilate, was crucified, died,
and was buried; He descended into hell; on the third day
He rose again from the dead; He ascended into heaven and
is seated at the right hand of God, the Father almighty;
from there He will come to judge the living and the dead.
I believe in the Holy Spirit, the holy Catholic Church, the
communion of saints, the forgiveness of sins, the resurrection of the body, and life everlasting. Amen.

Our Father

Our Father, who art in heaven, hallowed be Thy name.
Thy kingdom come. Thy will be done on earth as it is in
heaven. Give us this day our daily bread, and forgive us

our trespasses, as we forgive those who trespass against us. And lead us not into temptation, but deliver us from evil. Amen.

Hail Mary

Hail Mary, full of grace, the Lord is with thee. Blessed art thou among women, and blessed is the fruit of thy womb, Jesus. Holy Mary, Mother of God, pray for us sinners, now and at the hour of our death. Amen.

Glory Be

Glory be to the Father, and to the Son, and to the Holy Spirit. As it was in the beginning is now, and ever shall be, world without end. Amen.

Fátima Prayer

O my Jesus, forgive us our sins, save us from the fires of hell, lead all souls to heaven, especially those in most need of Your mercy.

Hail, Holy Queen

Hail, holy Queen, mother of mercy, our life, our sweetness, and our hope. To thee do we cry, poor banished children of Eve. To thee do we send up our sighs, mourning, and weeping in this valley of tears. Turn then, most gracious advocate, thine eyes of mercy toward us, and after this our exile, show us the blessed fruit of thy womb, Jesus. O clement, O loving, O sweet Virgin Mary.

V. Pray for us, O Holy Mother of God.

R. That we may be made worthy of the promises of Christ.

Prayers of the Rosary

Rosary Prayer

O God, whose only-begotten Son, by His life, death, and Resurrection, has purchased for us the rewards of eternal salvation, grant, we beseech Thee, that while meditating on these mysteries of the most holy Rosary of the Blessed Virgin Mary, we may both imitate what they contain and obtain what they promise, through Christ our Lord. Amen.

⚜

A Scriptural Rosary for Priests

⚜

First Joyful Mystery: The Annunciation

The Priest's Vocation to Holiness

Luke 1:30-32

"And the angel said to her, 'Do not be afraid, Mary, for you have found favor with God. And behold you will conceive in your womb and bear a son, and you shall call his name Jesus. He will be great, and will be called the Son of the Most High.'"

Reflection from *Pastores Dabo Vobis*, no. 20

"Priests are bound in a special way to strive for perfection, since they are consecrated to God in a new way by their ordination. They have become living instruments of Christ the eternal priest, so that through the ages they can accomplish his wonderful work of reuniting the whole human race with heavenly power."

Petition

Eternal Father, when the priest asks, "How can this be?" remind him of Your love and grace that will lead him through a life of sacrifice and perfection. In the face of his human weakness, teach him the humility of his holy Mother Mary, who relied on God's grace.

Help him to forsake whatever is contrary to his sanctification for love of You. Make him mindful of the undefiled High Priest, who called him to radiate the holiness of His Sacred Heart. Teach him to act, think, and judge as a priest who is chosen to serve, not to be served. Help him to see how desperately the world needs his witness of holiness.

We entrust the priest to the Immaculate Heart of Mary.

⚜

Second Joyful Mystery: The Visitation

The Priest Consecrated for Mission

Luke 1:39-42

"In those days Mary arose and went with haste into the hill country, to a city of Judah, and she entered the house of Zechariah and greeted Elizabeth. And when Elizabeth heard the greeting of Mary, the babe leaped in her womb; and Elizabeth was filled with the Holy Spirit, and she exclaimed with a loud cry, 'Blessed are you among women, and blessed is the fruit of your womb!'"

Reflection from *Pastores Dabo Vobis*, no. 24

"Consecration is for mission.... This was the case in Jesus's life. This was the case in the lives of the apostles and their successors. This was the case for the entire Church and within her for priests: All have received the Spirit as a gift and call to holiness in and through the carrying out of the mission. Therefore, an intimate bond exists between the priest's spiritual life and the exercise of his ministry."

A Scriptural Rosary for Priests

Petition

Eternal Father, kindly help the priest to understand that he is called to be Your faithful son.

When he professes that he belongs entirely to You, let his profession of love be real.

Move the heart of the priest to self-mortification and complete abandonment to the divine will. If he becomes occupied with worldly thoughts and ambitions, let him know that he is far from You.

Lead him to the fruitful fulfillment of his priestly mission, sanctifying him as he serves the faithful entrusted to him.

We entrust the priest to the Immaculate Heart of Mary.

༈

Third Joyful Mystery: The Birth of the Lord

The Priest, Shepherd

Luke 2:7

"And she gave birth to her first-born son and wrapped him in swaddling cloths, and laid him in a manger, because there was no place for them in the inn."

Reflection from *Pastores Dabo Vobis*, no. 22

"Jesus presents himself as 'the good shepherd' (Jn. 10:11, 14), not only of Israel but of all humanity (cf. Jn. 10:16). He feels compassion for the crowds because they were harassed and helpless, like sheep without a shepherd (cf. Mt. 9:35-36). He goes in search of the straying and scattered sheep (cf. Mt. 18:12-14) and joyfully celebrates their return. He gathers and protects them. He knows and calls each one by name (cf. Jn. 10:3). He leads them to green pastures and still waters (cf. Ps. 22-23) and spreads a table for them, nourishing them with his own life."

Petition

Eternal Father, grant that the priest be a good shepherd who never tires of looking for the straying and scattered sheep! Graciously help the priest to be like Jesus, who captures sinners with a look of agape charity, a whisper of truth, and a merciful invitation to something far better, to come back to the Church's table, where the Good Shepherd feeds them His life at the altar He prepared for their salvation.

We entrust the priest to the Immaculate Heart of Mary.

✲

Fourth Joyful Mystery:
The Presentation of the Lord

The Priest's Gift of Self

Luke 2:22-24

"And when the time came for their purification according to the law of Moses, they brought him up to Jerusalem to present him to the Lord ... and to offer a sacrifice according to what is said in the law of the Lord, 'a pair of turtledoves, or two young pigeons.'"

Reflection from *Pastores Dabo Vobis*, no. 23

"The gift of self, which is the source and synthesis of pastoral charity, is directed toward the Church. This was true of Christ who 'loved the Church and gave himself up for her' (Eph. 5:25), and the same must be true for the priest. Only by directing every moment and every one of his acts toward the fundamental choice to 'give his life for the flock' can the priest guarantee this unity which is vital and indispensable for his harmony and spiritual balance."

Petition

Eternal Father, I beg You to help the priest believe that he possesses the celestial treasure of Christ, who loved him first. May the priest cry out, "You are my ideal, Jesus! You are not some ideal forged by human imagination; You supersede all that the human mind can comprehend. I donate myself to You and the Church, imitating Your life of divine love, purity, poverty, zeal, preaching, miracles, agonizing desolation, the Cross, and the triumph of Your Resurrection. Only in, with, and through You can I say, 'I give my life for the flock.' "

We entrust the priest to the Immaculate Heart of Mary.

⚜

Fifth Joyful Mystery: The Finding of the Child Jesus in the Temple

The Priest, Minister of the Word

Luke 2:46-47

"After three days [Joseph and Mary] found him in the temple, sitting among the teachers, listening to them and asking them questions; and all who heard him were amazed at his understanding and his answers."

Reflection from *Pastores Dabo Vobis*, no. 26

"The priest is first of all a minister of the word of God. He needs to approach the word with a docile and prayerful heart so that it may deeply penetrate his thoughts and feelings and bring about a new outlook rooted in 'the mind of Christ' (1 Cor. 2:16) — such that his words, choices and attitudes may become ever more a reflection, a proclamation and a witness to the Gospel. Only if he 'abides' in the word will the priest become a perfect disciple of the Lord. Only then will he know the truth and be truly set free."

Petition

Father, You place the priest in Your house to be transformed into the living Word. You make him a minister of the Word for the Church. Help the priest to grasp the "conditions and demands, the manifestations and fruits of the intimate bond between [his] spiritual life and the exercise of his threefold ministry of word, sacrament and pastoral charity" (Pastores Dabo Vobis, no. 26).

Open the ears of the priest so that he hears Jesus saying, "You are not alone. Abide in my word."

We entrust the priest to the Immaculate Heart of Mary.

༺

First Sorrowful Mystery:
The Agony in the Garden

Priestly Obedience

Matthew 26:36-39

"Then Jesus went with them to a place called Gethsemane, and he said to his disciples, 'Sit here, while I go yonder and pray.' And taking with him Peter and the two sons of Zebedee, he began to be sorrowful and troubled. Then he said to them, 'My soul is very sorrowful, even to death; remain here, and watch with me.' And going a little farther he fell on his face and prayed, 'My Father, if it be possible, let this cup pass from me; nevertheless, not as I will, but as thou wilt.'"

Reflection from *Pastores Dabo Vobis,* no. 28

"It is in the spiritual life of the priest that obedience takes on certain special characteristics. First of all, obedience is indeed 'apostolic' in the sense that it recognizes, loves and serves the Church in her hierarchical structure. Priestly obedience has a particular 'pastoral' character. It is lived in an atmosphere of constant readiness to allow oneself to be taken up, as it were 'consumed,' by the needs and demands of the flock."

Petition

Eternal Father, Your Son is the icon of obedience. Generously dispose the priest to say, "Let me glorify You with the gift of my free will." Priestly obedience invites humility and provides for the fulfillment of Your holy plan for the priest and the Church. Let nothing on earth cause him to compromise his promise of obedience, which helps him to disappear from his own sight, not having any other will but that of Jesus.

Bless the obedient priest-son who prays, "May my heart be a canvas of humility, mortification, penance, self-denial, surrender, silence, and obedience according to my Heavenly Father's will, for He loves me."

We entrust the priest to the Immaculate Heart of Mary.

⚜

Second Sorrowful Mystery:
The Scourging at the Pillar

The Priest Configured to Christ

Matthew 27:24-26

"So when Pilate saw that he was gaining nothing, but rather that a riot was beginning, he took water and washed his hands before the crowd, saying, 'I am innocent of this righteous man's blood; see to it yourselves.' And all the people answered, 'His blood be on us and on our children!' Then he released for them Barabbas, and having scourged Jesus, delivered him to be crucified."

Reflection from *Pastores Dabo Vobis*, no. 21

"Jesus Christ is the head of the Church his body. He is the 'head' in the new and unique sense of being a 'servant', according to his own words: 'The Son of Man came not to be served but to serve, and to give his life as a ransom for many' (Mk. 10:45). Jesus's service attains its fullest expression in his death on the cross, that is, in this total gift of self in humility and love."

Petition

Eternal Father, graciously empower the priest to discover the joy of being configured to Christ even in the sharing of Christ's desolation during the scourging at the pillar, when He healed humanity by His stripes. Help the priest to sacrifice his comfort but not his honor, to live humbly in hope and never despair in the face of unjust persecution exerted on him by a cynical world. May his expectations conform to the divine expectation, always simple, equitable, patient, and charitable.

We entrust the priest to the Immaculate Heart of Mary.

ᴊ

Third Sorrowful Mystery:
The Crowning with Thorns

The Priest and Confession

Matthew 27:27-30

"Then the soldiers of the governor took Jesus into the praetorium, and they gathered the whole battalion before him. And they stripped him and put a scarlet robe upon him, and plaiting a crown of thorns they put it on his head, and put a reed in his right hand. And kneeling before him they mocked him saying, 'Hail, King of the Jews!' And they spat upon him, and took the reed and struck him on the head."

Reflection from *Pastores Dabo Vobis*, no. 26

"The priest's celebration of the Eucharist and administration of the other sacraments, his pastoral zeal, his relationship with the faithful, his communion with his brother priests, his collaboration with his bishop, his life of prayer — in a word, the whole of his priestly existence, suffers an inexorable decline if by negligence or for some other reason he fails to receive the sacrament of penance at regular intervals and in a spirit of genuine faith and devotion. If a priest were no longer to go to confession or properly confess his sins, his priestly being and his priestly action would feel its effects very soon, and this would also be noticed by the community of which he was the pastor."

Petition

Eternal Father, help the priest to make himself accountable to a confessor. Make the soul of the priest sensitive to sin so he will quickly seek the means of forgiveness. Aid him to be a good penitent and, in turn, a good confessor. When he is united to Christ, he will feel the weight of his sins and those of others. He will suffer as Jesus did at the hands of sinners. Provide the necessary grace so that he may respond as Jesus did—with selfless love and mercy.

We entrust the priest to the Immaculate Heart of Mary.

⁂

Fourth Sorrowful Mystery:
Jesus Carries His Cross

The Priest's Relationship with Christ, Mediator

Matthew 27:31-32
"And when they [the Roman soldiers] had mocked him, they stripped him of the robe, and put his own clothes on him, and led him away to crucify him. As they were marching out, they came upon a man of Cyrene, Simon by name; this man they compelled to carry his cross."

Reflection from *Pastores Dabo Vobis*, no. 13
"Jesus brought his role as mediator to complete fulfillment when he offered himself on the cross, thereby opening to us, once and for all, access to the heavenly sanctuary, to the Father's house (cf. Heb. 9:24-28).... With the one definitive sacrifice of the cross, Jesus communicated to all his disciples the dignity and mission of the priests of the new and eternal covenant."

Petition
Eternal Father, Your Son freely carried His Cross, but He needed the help of Simon, who was compelled into service. Jesus

also accepted the spiritual aid of His Mother, who accompanied Him on the way of the Cross.

As the priest carries his cross daily in service to the Church, let him experience the presence of Mary and the welcomed service of the faithful chosen by You. Do not let the weight of his cross crush his spirit, even though it may break his heart. At the end of each day, when the priest is in the silence and solitude of his room, grant him peace and lead him to surrender the burdens of his ministry, laying them at the foot of the Cross.

We confide the priest to the Immaculate Heart of Mary.

⚜

Fifth Sorrowful Mystery:
The Crucifixion of Our Lord

The Priest's Self-Emptying

Matthew 27:33-37

"And when they came to a place called Golgotha (which means the place of the skull), they offered him wine to drink, mingled with gall; but when he tasted it, he would not drink it. And when they had crucified him, they divided his garments among them by casting lots; then they sat down and kept watch over him there. And over his head they put the charge against him, which read, 'This is Jesus the King of the Jews.'"

Reflection from *Pastores Dabo Vobis*, no. 30

"Jesus Christ, who brought his pastoral charity to perfection on the cross with a complete exterior and interior emptying of self, is both the model and source of the virtues of obedience, chastity and poverty which the priest is called to live out as an expression of his pastoral charity for his brothers and sisters."

Petition
Eternal Father, the priest, aware of his weakness, may say, "I am lacking in faith, hope, and love. I am rich only in humiliation, scorn, and disdain." Or perhaps the priest is tempted to live the pride of life instead of picking up his cross daily.

Protect him from Satan, who strategizes to destroy his vocation completely, tempting him to the extremes of discouragement and doubt and then to pride and vanity.

We entrust the priest to the Immaculate Heart of Mary.

⚜

First Glorious Mystery: The Resurrection
The Priest Renewed

John 20:15-16
"Jesus said to her, 'Woman, why are you weeping? Whom do you seek?' Supposing him to be the gardener, she said to him, 'Sir, if you have carried him away, tell me where you have laid him, and I will take him away.' Jesus said to her, 'Mary.' She turned and said to him in Hebrew, 'Rabboni!' (which means Teacher).

Reflection from *Pastores Dabo Vobis*, no. 33
"Renew in them the outpouring of your spirit of holiness: 'The Spirit of the Lord is upon me, because he has anointed me to preach good news to the poor' (Lk. 4:18). Indeed, our faith reveals to us the presence of the spirit of Christ at work in our being, in our acting and in our living, just as the sacrament of

orders has configured, equipped and molded it. Yes, the Spirit of the Lord is the principal agent in our spiritual life."

Petition

Eternal Father, aid the priest to hear the voice of Jesus confirming his vocation with subtle yet tangible signs.

Father, grant the priest Your paternal blessing and affirmation so that he might experience the security that comes from knowing he is a beloved son of a Father who never turns His back. Let the Easter miracle that makes all things new be at work in the heart of the priest.

We entrust the priest to the Immaculate Heart of Mary.

✿

Second Glorious Mystery: The Ascension

The Priest's Intimacy with God

Luke 24:49-51

"'And behold, I send the promise of my Father upon you; but stay in the city, until you are clothed with power from on high.' Then he led them out as far as Bethany, and lifting up his hands he blessed them. While he blessed them, he parted from them and was carried up into heaven."

Reflection from *Pastores Dabo Vobis*, no. 33

"The priestly vocation is essentially a call to holiness in the form which derives from the sacrament of orders. Holiness is intimacy with God; it is the imitation of Christ, who was poor, chaste and humble; it is unreserved love for souls and a giving of oneself on their behalf and for their true good; it is love for the Church which is holy and wants us to be holy, because this is the mission that Christ entrusted to her."

Petition

Eternal Father, please help the priest to remember that Jesus calls him "friend." Any friendship involves joys and sorrows, both of which are part of intimacy. How is he to know authentic intimacy with Jesus? He must not pray merely to get through his prayers but must pray from the heart. In Your great love, lead the priest into the Sacred Heart, where intimacy is found, identity revealed, and friendship enjoyed.

We entrust the priest to the Immaculate Heart of Mary.

✴

Third Glorious Mystery:
The Descent of the Holy Spirit at Pentecost

The Priest and Charisms

Acts 2:1-4

"When the day of Pentecost had come, they were all together in one place. And suddenly a sound came from heaven like the rush of a mighty wind, and it filled all the house where they were sitting. And there appeared to them tongues as of fire, distributed and resting on each one of them. And they were all filled with the Holy Spirit."

Reflection from *Pastores Dabo Vobis*, no. 31

"For the abundance of The Spirit's gifts to be welcomed with joy and allowed to bear fruit for the glory of God and the good of the entire Church, each person is required first to have a knowledge and discernment of his or her own charisms and those of others, and always to use these charisms with Christian humility, with firm self-control and with the intention, above all else, to help build up the entire community which each particular charism is meant to serve."

Petition

Eternal Father, we pray for the priest to become attuned to the movement of the Holy Spirit within his heart and ministry. Graciously help him to develop true devotion to the Holy Spirit. May the priest experience the grace of Pentecost in a personal way and so be filled with joy!

Help the priest to use his gifts well and to discern his charisms and those of others who are to help him in his priestly ministry.

We entrust the priest to the Immaculate Heart of Mary.

༈

Fourth Glorious Mystery:
The Assumption of Mary into Heaven

The Priest, Mary, and Poverty

Mary's Assumption is not explicitly recorded in Scripture. However, Pope Pius XII formally defined the Dogma of the Assumption in his apostolic constitution *Munificentissimus Deus* on November 1, 1950: "The Immaculate Mother of God, the ever Virgin Mary, having completed the course of her earthly life, was assumed body and soul into heavenly glory" (no. 44).

Praying for Priests

Reflection from *Pastores Dabo Vobis*, no. 30
"Priests, following the example of Christ, who, rich though he was, became poor for love of us (cf. 2 Cor. 8:9)—should consider the poor and weakest as people entrusted in a special way to them, and they should be capable of witnessing to poverty with a simple and austere lifestyle, having learned the generous renunciation of superfluous things."

Petition
Eternal Father, we pray for the priest to embrace a life of simplicity, as did Mary during her earthly sojourn. By Your grace, the priest can be an icon of simplicity in a world complicated by selfish greed and excessive materialism. Help the priest to become a signpost that points to the generous renunciation of superfluous things. Grant him the grace of interior freedom that is safeguarded and nourished by evangelical poverty.

May the priest truly model Christ's poverty and trust that You will provide what he needs daily. Bless him in his poverty and make him rich in faith, hope, and love.

We entrust the priest to the Immaculate Heart of Mary.

⁂

**Fifth Glorious Mystery:
The Coronation of Mary as Queen**

The Priest, Mary, and Celibacy

Revelation 12:1
"And a great portent appeared in heaven, a woman clothed with the sun, with the moon under her feet, and on her head a crown of twelve stars."

A Scriptural Rosary for Priests

Reflection from *Pastores Dabo Vobis*, no. 29

"Priestly celibacy, then, is the gift of self in and with Christ to his Church and expresses the priest's service to the Church in and with the Lord.... Celibacy, then, is to be welcomed and continually renewed with a free and loving decision as a priceless gift from God, as an incentive to pastoral charity, as a singular sharing in God's fatherhood and in the fruitfulness of the Church."

Petition

Eternal Father, we pray that Mary will accompany the priest on the road to holiness and that she, who is utterly pure with celestial innocence, will stand guard over his gift of celibacy.

Help the priest to recognize that celibacy does not lead him to isolation or loneliness but creates more room within him to welcome the Church's entire family. Open his heart to share in Your Fatherhood, which creates more children for the glory of the eternal Kingdom.

We entrust the priest to the Immaculate Heart of Mary.

✣

First Luminous Mystery:
The Baptism of Our Lord

The Priest Servant

Matthew 3:16-17

"And when Jesus was baptized, he went up immediately from the water, and behold, the heavens were opened and he saw the Spirit of God descending like a dove, and alighting on him; and lo, a voice from heaven, saying, 'This is my beloved Son, with whom I am well pleased.'"

Reflection from *Pastores Dabo Vobis*, no. 23

"Above all, this was the explicit and programmatic teaching of Jesus when he entrusted to Peter the ministry of shepherding the flock only after his threefold affirmation of love, indeed only after he had expressed a preferential love: 'He said to him the third time, "Simon, son of John, do you love me?" Peter ... said to him, "Lord, you know everything; you know that I love you." Jesus said to him, "Feed my sheep." ' (Jn. 21:17)."

Petition

Eternal Father, bless the priest with Your fatherly affirmation, and speak to his heart the words he longs to hear: "You are my beloved son, with whom I am well pleased."

Bless him that he will know who he is in Your sight. Help him to benefit from the continuous release of sacramental grace, especially baptismal grace, through which his innocence was restored, and the grace of Holy Orders, through which he was anointed to be an alter Christus. Grant him courage in pouring out his life and sacrificing his will for the needs of those he serves.

We entrust the priest to the Immaculate Heart of Mary.

⁂

Second Luminous Mystery:
Jesus's Self-Manifestation at the Wedding at Cana

The Priest as Missionary

John 2:3-5

"When the wine failed, the mother of Jesus said to him, 'They have no wine.' And Jesus said to her, 'O woman, what have you to do with me? My hour has not yet come.' His mother said to the servants, 'Do whatever he tells you.' "

Reflection from *Pastores Dabo Vobis*, no. 32

"All priests must have the mind and heart of missionaries open to the needs of the Church and the world, with concern for those farthest away and especially for the non-Christian groups in their area. They should have at heart, in their prayers and particularly at the Eucharistic sacrifice, the concern of the whole Church for all of humanity" (quoting *Redemptoris Missio*, no. 67).

Petition

Eternal Father, the glorious miracle at Cana manifests the magnanimity, obedience, and humility of Jesus, whose heart is always engaged in missionary zeal. Conformed to the heart of Jesus, the priest can expand his mind and heart to reach lovingly around the globe.

Help the priest to discern the gentle nudge of his Mother Mary, who will prompt him to act with the Holy Spirit. Through Mary's maternal intercession, may he become a vessel of miracles so that people will come back to the Church and believe!

We entrust the priest to the Immaculate Heart of Mary.

༒

**Third Luminous Mystery:
The Proclamation of the Kingdom of God**

The Priest and the Proclamation of the Gospel

Mark 1:14-15

"Now after John was arrested, Jesus came into Galilee, preaching the gospel of God, and saying, 'The time is fulfilled, and the kingdom of God is at hand; repent, and believe in the gospel.'"

Praying for Priests

Reflection from *Pastores Dabo Vobis*, no. 27

"For all Christians without exception, the radicalism of the Gospel represents a fundamental, undeniable demand flowing from the call of Christ to follow and imitate him by virtue of the intimate communion of life with him brought about by the Spirit (cf. Mt 8:18ff.; 10:37ff.; Mk 8:34-38; 10:17-21; Lk 9:57ff.). This same demand is made anew to priests, not only because they are 'in' the Church, but because they are 'in the forefront' of the Church inasmuch as they are configured to Christ, the head and shepherd, equipped for and committed to the ordained ministry, and inspired by pastoral charity."

Petition

Eternal Father, if the priest is met with criticism when he proclaims the gospel, support him so that nothing will smother his zeal for the truth. Let the faithful see in their priest the harmony of what he says and lives. Transform the mind and heart of the priest so that his only proclamation is that of Jesus and the Church.

We entrust the priest to the Immaculate Heart of Mary.

⸙

Fourth Luminous Mystery:
The Transfiguration of Our Lord

The Priest and Divine Love

Matthew 17:2-6

"He was transfigured before them, and his face shone like the sun, and his garments became as white as light. And behold, there appeared to them Moses and Elijah, talking with him. And

Peter said to Jesus, 'Lord, it is well that we are here; if you wish, I will make three booths here, one for you and one for Moses and one for Elijah.' He was speaking when lo, a bright cloud overshadowed them, and a voice from the cloud said, 'This is my beloved Son, with whom I am well pleased; listen to him.' When the disciples heard this, they fell on their faces and were filled with awe."

Reflection from *Pastores Dabo Vobis*, no. 25

"Jesus first asks Peter if he loves him so as to be able to entrust his flock to him. However, in reality it was Christ's own love, free and unsolicited, which gave rise to his question to Peter and to his act of entrusting 'his' sheep to Peter. Therefore, every ministerial action—while it leads to loving and serving the Church—provides an incentive to grow in ever greater love and service of Jesus Christ the head, shepherd and spouse of the Church, a love which is always a response to the free and unsolicited love of God in Christ."

Petition

Eternal Father, I beg You to allow the priest to experience Your healing Love; wrap him in the security of the Trinitarian embrace. Help the priest to respond with profound gratitude that he is Your son, chosen and loved by You.

May a ray of the celestial light that Peter, James, and John saw during the Transfiguration pierce the priest, confirm his vocation, and strengthen him to be a light in the darkness.

We entrust the priest to the Immaculate Heart of Mary.

⚜

Fifth Luminous Mystery:
The Institution of the Holy Eucharist

The Priest and the Eucharist

Matthew 26:26-28
"Now as they were eating, Jesus took bread, and blessed, and broke it, and gave it to the disciples and said, 'Take, eat; this is my body.' And he took a cup, and when he had given thanks he gave it to them, saying, 'Drink of it, all of you; for this is my blood of the covenant, which is poured out for many for the forgiveness of sins.'"

Reflection from *Pastores Dabo Vobis*, no. 23
"Indeed, the Eucharist re-presents, makes once again present, the sacrifice of the cross, the full gift of Christ to the Church, the gift of his body given and his blood shed, as the supreme witness of the fact that he is head and shepherd, servant and spouse of the Church."

Petition
Eternal Father, preserve the priest from offending the Lamb who, at the altar, becomes vulnerable in the priest's anointed hands. May the crimson cloak of the Precious Blood be for the priest his mystical vestment of glory and joy. May the Eucharist be his consolation always!

We entrust the priest to the Immaculate Heart of Mary.

*

The Luminous Mysteries of the Rosary
for Vocations

As you offer this Rosary for vocations to the priesthood, I invite
you to join your prayers to the following prayer of Pope Emeritus
Benedict XVI:

*O Father, raise up among Christians abundant and holy
vocations to the priesthood, who keep the faith alive and
guard the blessed memory of your Son Jesus through the
preaching of the Word and the administration of the Sacraments, with which you continually renew your faithful.*

*Grant us holy ministers of your altar, who are careful
and fervent guardians of the Eucharist, the sacrament of
the supreme gift of Christ for the redemption of the world.
Call ministers of your mercy, who, through the sacrament of
Reconciliation, spread the joy of your forgiveness.*

*Grant, O Father, that the Church may welcome with
joy the numerous inspirations of the Spirit of your Son and,
docile to His teachings, may she care for vocations to the
ministerial priesthood and to the consecrated life.*

*Sustain bishops, priests and deacons, consecrated men
and women, and all the baptized in Christ, so that they*

may faithfully fulfill their mission at the service of the Gospel.
This we pray through Christ our Lord. Amen.
Mary, Queen of Apostles, pray for us.[113]

꙳

THE LUMINOUS MYSTERIES

First Luminous Mystery:
The Baptism of Our Lord

Vocations: Come and See

Matthew 3:16-17
"And when Jesus was baptized, he went up immediately from the water, and behold, the heavens were opened and he saw the Spirit of God descending like a dove, and alighting on him; and lo, a voice from heaven, saying, 'This is my beloved Son, with whom I am well pleased.'"

Reflection from *Pastores Dabo Vobis*, no. 34
"By the very fact that 'the lack of priests is certainly a sad thing for any Church,' pastoral work for the vocation needs especially today, to be taken up with a new vigor and more decisive commitment by all the members of the Church, in the awareness that it is not a secondary or marginal matter, or the business of one

[113] Pope Benedict XVI, Prayer for Vocations for the 43rd World Day of Prayer for Vocations, quoted in United States Conference of Catholic Bishops, *Catholic Household Blessings and Prayers* (Washington, D.C.: United States Conference of Catholic Bishops, 2007), 385-386.

group only, as if it were but a 'part,' no matter how important, of the entire pastoral work of the Church."

Petition

Eternal Father, we implore Your paternal heart to let the floodgates of grace open for an increase of vocations to the ministerial priesthood. May couples be open to life and know the blessing of children. May Catholic families be inspired to pray together and parents be led to encourage their sons to seriously consider the priesthood. Graciously touch the hearts of young men to respond to the mysterious invitation of Jesus: "Come, follow me" (Matt. 19:21) and "Come and see" (John 1:39).

We entrust this intention to the Immaculate Heart of Mary.

⚜

Second Luminous Mystery:
Jesus's Self-Manifestation at the Wedding at Cana

The Church and the Gift of Vocations

John 2:3-5

"When the wine failed, the mother of Jesus said to him, 'They have no wine.' And Jesus said to her, 'O woman, what have you to do with me? My hour has not yet come.' His mother said to the servants, 'Do whatever he tells you.'"

Reflection from *Pastores Dabo Vobis,* no. 35

"What is true of every vocation is true specifically of the priestly vocation: the latter is a call, by the sacrament of holy orders received in the Church, to place oneself at the service of the

People of God with a particular belonging and configuration to Jesus Christ and with the authority of acting 'in the name and in the person' of him who is head and shepherd of the Church."

Petition

Eternal Father, deign to bring forth more priestly vocations to address the serious and urgent needs that confront the Church and the world.

Open our eyes to recognize vocations that are budding in young men so that communities of faith may nurture them. Touch the hearts of young men, and enable them to go out into the world as alteri Christi to proclaim to humanity the truth of the gospel.

May the Mother of Jesus, full of wisdom and grace, help raise many young men to follow in the footsteps of her Son, Jesus, the Eternal High Priest!

We entrust all young men discerning a vocation to the Immaculate Heart of Mary.

⚜

Third Luminous Mystery:
The Proclamation of the Kingdom of God

Divine Will and Human Response

Mark 1:16-17

"Passing along by the Sea of Galilee, he saw Simon and Andrew the brother of Simon casting a net in the sea; for they were fishermen. And Jesus said to them, 'Follow me, and I will make you become fishers of men.'"

The Luminous Mysteries of the Rosary for Vocations

Reflection from *Pastores Dabo Vobis*, no. 36

"God's free and sovereign decision to call man calls for total respect. It cannot be forced in the slightest by any human ambition, and it cannot be replaced by any human decision. Vocation is a gift of God's grace and never a human right, such that 'one can never consider priestly life as a simply human affair, nor the mission of the minister as a simply personal project.' Every claim or presumption on the part of those called is thus radically excluded (cf. Heb. 5:4 ff.). Their entire heart and spirit should be filled with an amazed and deeply felt gratitude, and unshakable trust and hope, because those who have been called know that they are rooted not in their own strength but in the unconditional faithfulness of God who calls."

Petition

Eternal Father, we pray that You protect the seminarian in Your paternal love. Grant him magnanimity of heart, stamina for the mission, affinity for the interior life, adaptability to his environment, and fraternity with his fellow seminarians. In Your kindness, anoint his intellect for the rigors of academics, reveal his true identity to him, keep his intentions pure, heal any wounds that need to be cured, and equip him with charisms to glorify You and build up the Church.

Protect him from pride and self-reliance. Free him from himself and from disordered appetites that would hinder his total transformation in Christ.

We entrust the seminarian to the Immaculate Heart of Mary.

⚜

Fourth Luminous Mystery:
The Transfiguration of Our Lord

Pastoral Work for Promoting Vocations

Matthew 17:2-5

"He was transfigured before them, and his face shone like the sun, and his garments became as white as light. And behold, there appeared to them Moses and Elijah, talking with him. And Peter said to Jesus, 'Lord, it is well that we are here; if you wish, I will make three booths here, one for you and one for Moses and one for Elijah.' He was speaking when lo, a bright cloud overshadowed them, and a voice from the cloud said, 'This is my beloved Son, with whom I am well pleased; listen to him.'"

Reflection from *Pastores Dabo Vobis*, no. 38

"The Church, as a priestly, prophetic and kingly people, is committed to foster and to serve the birth and maturing of priestly vocations through her prayer and sacramental life; by her proclamation of the word and by education in the faith; by her example and witness of charity."

Petition

Eternal Father, set the Church ablaze with intercessory prayer for the men who have yet to discern the call to priesthood and also for seminarians, transitional deacons, and men about to be ordained. Surround and protect them with the prayers of the faithful.

We entrust them all to the Immaculate Heart of Mary.

ᴥ

Fifth Luminous Mystery:
The Institution of the Holy Eucharist

We Are All Responsible for Promoting Vocations

Matthew 26:26-28

"Now as they were eating, Jesus took bread, and blessed, and broke it, and gave it to the disciples and said, 'Take, eat; this is my body.' And he took a cup, and when he had given thanks he gave it to them, saying, 'Drink of it, all of you; for this is my blood of the covenant, which is poured out for many for the forgiveness of sins.'"

Reflection from *Pastores Dabo Vobis*, no. 41

"The priestly vocation is a gift from God. The Church, therefore, is called to safeguard this gift, to esteem it and love it. She is responsible for the birth and development of priestly vocations.... There is an urgent need, especially nowadays, for a more widespread and deeply felt conviction that all the members of the Church, without exception, have the grace and responsibility to look after vocations."

Petition

Eternal Father, through the Eucharistic life of the Church, stir the heart of a future priest to fall in love with Christ in an absolute and final way. Through the Eucharist, seize the imagination of young men for Christ. Through the Eucharist, heal the deafness, blindness, stubbornness, selfishness, and wounds that could divert his attraction to the priesthood. Through the Eucharist, gently lead him to a future place of certitude, joy, and humility where he can say the words, "Take, eat; this is my body."

A Prayerful Response to Clergy Scandals: The Rosary of Reparation

Every Holy Thursday, Pope John Paul II would address all priests of the universal Church by letter. In his message for March 17, 2002, he wrote the following:

> At this time, as priests we are personally and profoundly afflicted by the sins of some of our brothers who have betrayed the grace of Ordination in succumbing even to the most grievous forms of the *mysterium iniquitatis* at work in the world. Grave scandal is caused, with the result that a dark shadow of suspicion is cast over all the other fine priests who perform their ministry with honesty and integrity and often with heroic self-sacrifice. As the Church shows her concern for the victims and strives to respond in truth and justice to each of these painful situations, all of us—conscious of human weakness, but trusting in the healing power of divine grace—are called *to embrace the "mysterium Crucis"* and to commit ourselves more fully to the search for holiness. We must beg God in his Providence to prompt a whole-hearted reawakening of those

ideals of total self-giving to Christ which are the very foundation of the priestly ministry. (no. 11)

The *Catechism* teaches the following about scandal: "Scandal is an attitude or behavior which leads another to do evil. The person who gives scandal becomes his neighbor's tempter. He damages virtue and integrity; he may even draw his brother into spiritual death" (no. 2284).

There is a need for both reparation and healing. St. James tells us: "Pray for one another, that you may be healed" (5:16).

Some of our greatest joys and also some of our deepest pain occur from relationships within the Church precisely because we are a spiritual family, one body in Christ (cf. 1 Cor. 12:12). But our condition is worse if we separate from God's family.

As you pray this Rosary of Reparation, I hope you will take comfort from these words by Sister Lucía of Fátima: "From the moment that Our Lady gave importance to the Rosary, there is no problem, material or spiritual, national or international, which cannot be solved."[114] I also invite you to ask the eternal Father to draw you, the pope, the bishops, the priests, and all the laity, especially victims of abuse, deeper into the redeeming love of the Passion of His Son, Jesus Christ. May we experience the healing power of divine love, as the prophet Isaiah teaches:

> Surely he has borne our griefs and carried our sorrows; yet we esteemed him stricken, smitten by God, and afflicted. But he was wounded for our transgressions, he was bruised

[114] Quoted in Stefano M. Manelli, *Devotion to Our Lady: The Marian Life as Taught by the Saints* (New Bedford, MA: Academy of the Immaculate, 2001), 141.

for our iniquities; upon him was the chastisement that
made us whole, and with his stripes we are healed. All we
like sheep have gone astray; we have turned every one to
his own way; and the LORD has laid on him the iniquity
of us all. (Isa. 53:4-6)

⚜

THE SORROWFUL MYSTERIES

First Sorrowful Mystery:
The Agony in the Garden

For Victims of Priest Abuse

Matthew 26:38-39

"Then he said to them, 'My soul is very sorrowful, even to
death; remain here, and watch with me.' And going a little
farther he fell on his face and prayed, 'My Father, if it be possible, let this cup pass from me; nevertheless, not as I will, but
as thou wilt.'"

Reflection from *Salvifici Dolores*, no. 9

"Within each form of suffering endured by man, and at the same
time at the basis of the whole world of suffering, there inevitably
arises *the question: why?* ... But only the suffering human being
knows what he is suffering and wonders why; and he suffers in a
humanly speaking still deeper way if he does not find a satisfac-
tory answer. This is a *difficult question*, just as is a question closely
akin to it, the question of evil. Why does evil exist? Why is
there evil in the world? When we put the question this way, we
are always, at least to a certain extent, asking a question about

suffering too.... Man can put this question to God with all the emotion of his heart and with his mind full of dismay and anxiety; and God expects the question and listens to it, as we see in ... the Book of Job."

Petition

Eternal Father, Your Son was sorrowful unto death during His agony in the Garden of Gethsemane, when the sins of the world pressed upon His innocent being until His sweat became blood. He endured the terror of human suffering, the tyranny of injustice and the horror of sin to redeem sinners.

We beg You to heal and bless the victims of priestly abuse who have shared a portion of the Passion of Jesus. We ask You to restore what was unjustly taken from the victims. We implore You to open the floodgates of mercy upon all victims for a renewal of their scarred memory, broken hearts, dishonored bodies, and inconsolable spirits. By Your loving grace, restore their lives.

We entrust all victims to our Sorrowful Mother, who held her suffering Son in her maternal arms and cleansed His wounds.

✤

Second Sorrowful Mystery: The Scourging at the Pillar

For Priests Who Hurt Others

Matthew 27:24-26

"So when Pilate saw that he was gaining nothing, but rather that a riot was beginning, he took water and washed his hands before the crowd, saying, 'I am innocent of this righteous man's blood; see to it yourselves.' And all the people answered, 'His blood be on us and on our children!' Then he released for them Barabbas, and having scourged Jesus, delivered him to be crucified."

Reflection from *Salvifici Dolores*, nos. 12-13

"Suffering must serve *for conversion*, that is, *for the rebuilding of goodness in the subject*, who can recognize the divine mercy in this call to repentance. The purpose of penance is to overcome evil, which under different forms lies dormant in man. Its purpose is also to strengthen goodness both in man himself and in his relationships with others and especially with God. But in order to perceive the true answer to the 'why' of suffering, we must look to the revelation of divine love, the ultimate source of the meaning of everything that exists. Love is also the richest source of the meaning of suffering, which always remains a mystery; we are conscious of the insufficiency and inadequacy of our explanations. Christ causes us to enter into the mystery and to discover the 'why' of suffering, as far as we are capable of grasping the sublimity of divine love."

Petition

Eternal Father, we bring before You the priests who have hurt others by some form of abuse. All have sinned and fall short of the glory of God (Rom. 3:23), but when a priest falls into sin and hurts a person entrusted to him, some goodness dies within the entire Body of Christ. Although the transgressions of some priests may be horrific and people cry out for vengeance, we entrust them to Your fatherly providence.

We entrust fallen priests to the heart of our Sorrowful Mother.

᙮

Third Sorrowful Mystery:
The Crowning with Thorns

For Falsely Accused Priests

Matthew 27:28-30

"And they stripped him and put a scarlet robe upon him, and plaiting a crown of thorns they put it on his head, and put a reed in his right hand. And kneeling before him they mocked him saying, 'Hail, King of the Jews!' And they spat upon him, and took the reed and struck him on the head."

Reflection from *Salvifici Dolores*, no. 16

"Christ drew close above all to the world of human suffering through the fact of having taken *this suffering upon his very self*. During his public activity, he experienced not only fatigue, homelessness, misunderstanding even on the part of those closest to him, but, more than anything, he became progressively more and more isolated and encircled by hostility and the preparations for putting him to death.... Christ goes towards his Passion and death with full awareness of the mission that he has to fulfill precisely in this way. Precisely *by means of this suffering* he must bring it about 'that man should not perish, but have eternal life.' Precisely by means of his Cross he must strike at the roots of evil, planted in the history of man and in human souls."

Petition

Eternal Father, we bring before Your throne of mercy the priests who have been wrongly accused and who, although innocent, are treated like outcasts and forsaken by many.

A Prayerful Response to Clergy Scandals

We ask You to console with paternal solicitude those priests who have been stripped of everything and are set apart like lepers, even though they are innocent of the charges against them. In Your mercy, graciously heal any wounds stemming from the experience of unfounded accusations — especially anger, depression, anxiety, loneliness, rejection, and fear. In Your justice, restore the good names of those who are innocent, and bring justice where it is needed.

We entrust all these priests to Mary, our Sorrowful Mother.

❧

Fourth Sorrowful Mystery:
Jesus Carries His Cross

For Healing

Matthew 27:31-32

"And when they [the Roman soldiers] had mocked him, they stripped him of the robe, and put his own clothes on him, and led him away to crucify him. As they were marching out, they came upon a man of Cyrene, Simon by name; this man they compelled to carry his cross."

Reflection from *Salvifici Dolores*, no. 16

"'For God so loved the world that he gave his only Son, that whoever believes in him should not perish but have eternal life.' Christ goes toward his own suffering, aware of its saving power; he goes forward in obedience to the Father, but primarily he is *united to the Father in this love* with which he has loved the world and man in the world. And for this reason St. Paul will write of Christ, 'He loved me and gave himself for me.'"

Praying for Priests

Petition

Eternal Father, the Body of Christ experiences the weight of scandal and persecution. We have corporately sinned against the greatest commandment of divine love. Graciously bring about a movement of medicinal reparation. Enkindle the hearts of the faithful to seek the healing balm of sacramental life. We trust that You will bring good out of the immense suffering of the Church as we humble ourselves before You. By the blood of the Lamb, cure our sin-sickness; take away our darkness, blindness, deafness, stubbornness, divisions, depression, sloth, vice, and pride. Through the Eucharist, may the Divine Physician manifest His healing power.

We entrust this petition to the heart of Mary, our Sorrowful Mother.

⚜

Fifth Sorrowful Mystery:
The Crucifixion of Our Lord

Forgiveness

Luke 23:34

"And Jesus said, 'Father, forgive them; for they know not what they do.' And they cast lots to divide his garments."

Reflection from *Salvifici Dolores*, no. 30

"In the messianic program of Christ, which is at the same time the program *of the Kingdom of God*, suffering is present in the world in order to release love, in order to give birth to works of love towards neighbor, in order to transform the whole of human civilization into a 'civilization of love.' ... At one and the same time Christ has taught man *to do good by his suffering* and *to do good to those who suffer*. In this double aspect he has completely revealed the meaning of suffering."

Petition

Eternal Father, before Your Son Jesus expired on the Cross, He offered the greatest gift of divine mercy, saying, "Father, forgive them, for they know not what they do." Help the faithful to offer forgiveness from the heart. Aid the Church in applying the healing salve of mercy to the deep wounds inflicted by scandal and persecution. Heal the anger and frustration of Your people who are mystified by what has happened in the Church. Only by Your grace can we be reconciled to each another and forgive as Jesus does Thank You for the many good servants who are working to heal those who suffer the scars of abuse.

Cleanse Your house of all that is defiled and dead. Through the grace of forgiveness, make us healthy and holy.

We entrust this petition to the heart of Mary, our Sorrowful Mother.[115]

---

[115] The Rosary of Reparation for Clergy Scandals is available as a printable trifold brochure at www.foundationforpriests.org.

⚜

Suggested Prayers and Offerings for Priests

⚜

St. Thérèse of the Child Jesus' Prayer for Priests

O Jesus, I pray for your faithful and fervent priests; for your unfaithful and tepid priests; for your priests laboring at home or abroad in distant mission fields; for your tempted priests; for your lonely and desolate priests; for your young priests; for your dying priests; for the souls of your priests in purgatory. But above all, I recommend to you the priests dearest to me: the priest who baptized me; the priests who absolved me from my sins; the priests at whose Masses I assisted and who gave me your Body and Blood in Holy Communion; the priests who taught and instructed me; all the priests to whom I am indebted in any other way (especially . . .). O Jesus, keep them all close to your heart, and bless them abundantly in time and in eternity. Amen.

⚜

A Spiritual Mother or Father's Self-Offering

Heavenly Father, I am inspired by the glorious witness of saints who went before me on the royal road of spiritual motherhood and fatherhood.[116] *I unite my offering to all the spiritual mothers and fathers of priests throughout the history of the Church. I pray that I can imitate their fidelity and fruitfulness in the handing down of the Faith to future generations.*

Eternal Father, graciously keep my heart set on this intention of praying and sacrificing for holy priests that they may be victorious over the world, the flesh, and the devil.

United with Jesus, I offer myself as an intercessor for priests in purgatory and for priests serving the Church now and in the future.

I beseech you to grant all priests and seminarians necessary grace to persevere in their ongoing formation and interior transformation.

When the priest holds the Sacred Host in his hands at the Holy Sacrifice of the Mass, grant that he may experience the love of the Most Holy Trinity enveloping him and be strengthened.

Heavenly Father, every time I see the priest elevating Your Son Jesus in the Eucharist, I renew and ratify my self-offering for priests. It is my ardent and constant desire that You be glorified through the holiness of your priests.

I confide my self-offering prayer to You through the Immaculate Heart of Mary.

✼

Seven Holy Communions for Priests

Your time of Holy Communion is an occasion of great intimacy with Jesus. By offering that graced moment for one or more priests, you deepen your spiritual motherhood or fatherhood while asking God to bless priests.

[116] In the spirit of the prophet Simeon and St. Joseph, men are encouraged to be spiritual fathers of priests also.

Suggested Prayers and Offerings for Priests

These Communions could be offered on seven consecutive days or on seven Sundays.

※

1. Jesus, by the grace of my Holy Communion, I beg You to send anew the Holy Spirit upon all priests for their sanctification. May they be the instruments that fulfill Your prayer, "I came to cast fire upon the earth; and would that it were already kindled!" (Luke 12:49).

※

2. Jesus, by the grace of my Holy Communion, I beg You to liberate priests who are suffering from any form of spiritual warfare. Send forth Your mighty word to bind and cast out any darkness that blocks their priestly fruitfulness.

※

3. Jesus, by the grace of my Holy Communion, I beg You to send forth an infusion of divine love upon the priest who needs it most. All human love is imperfect, but Your love is the healing balm for aching hearts. Look with favor upon the most desolate priest in the world, and reveal Your personal love to him.

※

4. Jesus, by the grace of my Holy Communion, I beg You to open the floodgates of divine mercy upon the priest who is in most need of the medicine of mercy. Graciously grant the priest the grace to accept it and become a vessel of divine mercy for others.

※

5. Jesus, by the grace of my Holy Communion, I beg You to infuse new priests with confident assurance of their vocational

calling. Graciously help them to navigate their mission and accept their assignments with docility and generosity. Build a brotherhood of virtuous priests, humble, joyful, and holy.

※

6. Jesus, by the grace of my Holy Communion, I beg You to bless all clergy with many spiritual children to worship You in spirit and truth. You chose and sent them to bear much fruit as spiritual fathers. Help them tend to their flocks without counting the cost and to be good, generous fathers spreading paternal charity throughout the Church.

※

7. Jesus, by the grace of my Holy Communion, I beg You to shower your saving grace upon _____ (insert the name of your pastor, parochial vicar, bishop, the Holy Father, or another priest who is on your heart). Please keep him safe in the refuge of the Immaculate Heart of Mary, who is his mother of grace. Grant him a deep and intimate prayer life to fuel all the demands of his priesthood. Please bless him with joy, peace, and generosity.

※

On Sanctification (for priests and their intercessors)
(Based on the *Anima Christi* prayer)

Soul of Christ, sanctify me: remove all that is unholy in my life. Sanctify me that I may glorify You.

Body of Christ, save me: from sin, the world, the devil, and myself. I renounce sin, the allurements of the world, and the lies of the devil.

Suggested Prayers and Offerings for Priests

Blood of Christ, inebriate me: fill me with the sober intoxication of the Spirit. Replace my sadness with joy, my anxiety with trust, my fear with love.

Water from the side of Christ, wash me: restore my baptismal innocence. Cleanse my impurities and clothe me in the purity of holiness.

Passion of Christ, strengthen me: secure me to the cross that I might die to myself. As I embrace the cross, I renounce the flesh.

O good Jesus, hear me: and let me hear *Your* voice guiding me. Keep me in Your love that I may listen and hear Your voice as You hear me.

Within Thy wounds, hide me: graciously heal me and transform me. Keep me safe within Your holy wounds and pierced heart.

Separated from Thee let me never be: if I wander away, seek and find me, Lord. Be my Good Shepherd and keep me in the flock that You guard.

From the malignant enemy, defend me: grant me wisdom to resist evil. In Your mercy, be my shield, sword, and strong armor.

At the hour of death, call me: prepare me to encounter You in death. May Mary accompany me through the portal to eternal life.

To come to Thee, bid me: never let me be parted from You, Lord. Call me to Your side; never let me go from Your embrace.

Praying for Priests

That I may praise Thee in the company of Thy saints, for all eternity: Let me see You face-to-face and glorify You forever.

Amen. I believe and I renounce my unbelief. *Amen.*

⁂

Seven Holy Hours for Priestly Virtues

This offering can be made on seven consecutive days or Sundays.

⁂

1. For priests to be blessed by an increase of expectant faith, constant hope, and fullness of love.

2. For priests to be blessed and grounded in the humility of the One Eternal High Priest, who lowered Himself to become the servant of all.

3. For priests to be blessed with the graces to faithfully live out their promise of celibacy for the sake of the Kingdom, which makes them fully available to serve their Bride, the Church, with single-hearted devotion.

4. For priests to be blessed with ever-increasing sanctity to shine the light of Trinitarian holiness upon the world.

5. For priests to be blessed with zeal for God and His Church; that they may have the dynamism of the Holy Spirit to animate their priesthood, especially their preaching.

6. For priests to be living examples of evangelical poverty and so be signposts for all members of the Church, who are called to be in the world but not of the world.

7. For priests to be endowed with the virtues of prudence, justice, and fortitude, that they might be other Christs who live

His spiritual martyrdom of love, especially through the daily offering of the Holy Sacrifice of the Mass.

⚜

For Priests and Bishops:
Litany of Reparation for Offenses against the Laity

For the times I have been condescending, impatient, or disrespectful toward the laity, *Lord, forgive me and have mercy.*

For the times I was unavailable to them through my own fault, *Lord, forgive me and have mercy.*

For the times I failed to encourage and support their good intentions, *Lord, forgive me and have mercy.*

For the times I put my comfort before their needs, *Lord, forgive me and have mercy.*

For the times I withdrew or hid myself for selfish reasons, *Lord, forgive me and have mercy.*

For the times I failed to communicate well the teachings of the Church, *Lord, forgive me and have mercy.*

For the times I failed to prepare well for my ministry, *Lord, forgive me and have mercy.*

For the times I failed to counsel or listen to the laity, *Lord, forgive me and have mercy.*

For the times I participated in gossip or slander directed at the laity, *Lord, forgive me and have mercy.*

For the times I caused scandal for the laity in any manner, *Lord, forgive me and have mercy.*

For the times I failed to pray for the laity or, through my negligence, failed to aid their growth in holiness, *Lord, forgive me and have mercy.* Amen.

Praying for Priests

✎

For Laity:
Litany of Reparation for Offenses
against the Priesthood

For the times we have not recognized or appreciated the valuable gift of the ministerial priesthood, *Lord, forgive us and have mercy.*

For the times we compete with priests, *Lord, forgive us and have mercy.*

For the times we thought our worth in the Church was compromised because of the ministerial priesthood, *Lord, forgive us and have mercy.*

For the ways we have not agreed with the teachings of the Church about priests, rebelled through our words and actions, or shown disrespect, *Lord, forgive us and have mercy.*

For the times we participated in gossip or slander directed at a priest, using our speech to tear down rather than to build up, *Lord, forgive us and have mercy.*

For allowing our anger over the abuse crisis to harden into suspicion toward all priests, *Lord, forgive us and have mercy.*

For the times we have behaved inappropriately toward priests, *Lord, forgive us and have mercy.*

For the times we neglected to pray and sacrifice for priests, *Lord, forgive us and have mercy.*

For the times we allowed our hearts to grow cold and critical and failed to treat priests with charity or gratitude, *Lord, forgive us and have mercy.*

Suggested Prayers and Offerings for Priests

For the times we have not forgiven priests and have withheld
mercy from them, *Lord, forgive us and have mercy.*
For the times we made selfish demands on priests while failing
to support them, *Lord, forgive us and have mercy.*
For the times we failed to pray for vocations or did not nurture
them in our children, *Lord, forgive us and have mercy.* Amen.

⚜

Praying for Priests Who Have Died

The Words of Jesus to Ven. Conchita

"I do not want to exclude priests who have died. They also
need prayers and suffrages so that they may return to my arms
from purgatory to heaven. Even there the mission of faithful
souls lasts, to free priests from that place of purification, to gain
for me the joy of seeing them finally in the bosom of my glory.
This will be an act of charity for them and a joy that they will
give Me....

"Many of my priests, almost all of them, do not give importance to this aspect of most important charity; and they leave
these intimate souls in the fire, without ever or very slightly
worrying about them.

"I want that in the memento of the departed at Mass, they
put their brother priests in the first place, without ever forgetting
them. This is my chosen portion and the joy that I experience
in receiving a priestly soul in heaven equals and even surpasses
greatly the love that I professed for them on earth....

"I succeeded in saving them with my very Blood, with tears
from my soul, with pleading groans to the Father, with my infinite merits; and they arise from the world contrite and pardoned.

Praying for Priests

"Then, when they are in purgatory, alas! now nothing is possible for them to do, but *wait*, wait that there are charitable souls that ransom them, lessen their pain and time."[117]

⁂

Petition for Priests in Purgatory

Most Holy Trinity, I offer my Holy Communion today for the priest in purgatory who has no one to pray for him. I beseech you to apply the unfathomable merits of the Eucharist I receive today to the priest in purgatory who is suffering the most. That I might console the Most Holy Trinity, I desire always to remember the souls in the place of purgation, most of all the souls of priests, who should never be forgotten. Finger of God, engrave on my intercessory heart this important petition, and accept my offering for love of the Eternal High Priest.

⁂

Offering of Suffering for Priests

My Savior Jesus, I do not comprehend the mystery of suffering, but I believe that it has a redemptive value when it is offered in union with Your Passion. I beseech You to accept the offering of all of my past, present, and future sufferings for the sanctification of priests, who are Your ministers of love. My suffering is small when compared with Your complete sacrifice of crucified love, but still I offer it to You. Please grant that through the daily offering of my suffering I can become a vessel of divine mercy for Your ministerial

---

[117] *To My Priests*, 239-240.

Suggested Prayers and Offerings for Priests

*priesthood. Please accept the offering of my suffering on their
behalf so they may become increasingly holy and zealous, wise and
humble, generous and pure.*

*Lord Jesus, take my suffering into Your holy wounds, and
through my offering, grant priests what they need for the greater
work of saving souls.*

*My Savior and Eternal High Priest, may my humble offering
console Your Sacred Heart.*

⸙

St. Faustina's Prayer for Priests

*"O my Jesus, I beg You on behalf of the whole Church: Grant
it love and the light of Your Spirit, and give power to the words of
Priests so that hardened hearts might be brought to repentance and
return to You, O Lord. Lord, give us holy Priests; You yourself
maintain them in holiness. O Divine and Great High Priest, may
the power of Your mercy accompany them everywhere and protect
them from the devil's traps and snares which are continually being
set for the soul of Priests.*

*"May the power of Your mercy, O Lord, shatter and bring to
naught all that might tarnish the sanctity of Priests, for You can do
all things" (Diary, no. 1052).*

⸙

Prayer of St. John Paul II to the Mother of Priests

*O Mary, Mother of Jesus Christ and Mother of priests, accept
this title which we bestow on you to celebrate your Motherhood and*

*to contemplate with you the priesthood of your Son and of your
sons, O holy Mother of God.*

*O Mother of Christ, to the Messiah-priest you gave a body of
flesh through the anointing of the Holy Spirit for the salvation of the
poor and the contrite of heart; guard priests in your heart and in the
Church, O Mother of the Savior.*

*O Mother of Faith, you accompanied to the Temple the Son
of Man, the fulfillment of the promises given to the fathers; give
to the Father for his glory the priests of your Son, O Ark of the
Covenant.*

*O Mother of the Church, in the midst of the disciples in the
upper room you prayed to the Spirit for the new people and their
shepherds; obtain for the Order of Presbyters, a full measure of
gifts, O Queen of the Apostles.*

*O Mother of Jesus Christ, you were with Him at the beginning
of his life and mission, you sought the Master among the crowd, you
stood beside him when he was lifted up from the earth, consumed
as the one eternal sacrifice, and you had John, your son, near at
hand; accept from the beginning those who have been called, protect
their growth, in their life ministry accompany your sons, O Mother
of Priests. Amen.*[118]

❧

Prayer for Vocations to the Priesthood and Religious Life

*O loving and gracious God, Father of all, You bless Your people
in every time and season and provide for their needs through Your
providential care. Your Church is continually in need of priests,*

---

[118] Pope John Paul II, *Pastores Dabo Vobis*, no. 82.

sisters, and brothers to offer themselves in the service of the gospel by lives of dedicated love. Open the hearts of Your sons and daughters to listen to Your call in their lives. Give them the gift of understanding to discern Your invitation to serve You and Your Church. Give them the gift of courage to follow Your call. May they have the spirit of young Samuel, who found fulfillment in his life when he said to You, "Speak Lord, for Your servant is listening." We ask this through Jesus Christ, our Lord and Redeemer. Amen.

⚜

Stations of the Cross for Priests and Laity

The First Station: Jesus Is Condemned to Death

Jesus stands before Pilate an innocent man, yet he is condemned to death. The pure Lamb of God is led to the slaughter and remains silent. He is intent on the mission and does not count the cost.

Eternal Father, graciously help our priests and us to avoid false judgments that are hurtful to Your Church. Grant that we never wash our hands of innocence, as did Pilate. We ask for the gift of courage for all priests. Please grant priests the grace to be faithful to their lofty mission.

The Second Station: Jesus Carries His Cross

Jesus, already tired and broken, picks up the heavy Cross to begin the journey to Calvary. Love compels Him. The weight of love is heavier than the Cross that tears into His shoulder.

Eternal Father, please help our priests and us when we are exhausted and overwhelmed by life and by our respective duties. For all priests, we ask for the gift of personal holiness that they may

*radiate the love the Sacred Heart of Jesus. Grant that love and
mercy will flow freely from the heart of priests.*

The Third Station: Jesus Falls the First Time
Jesus falls down under the weight of the heavy Cross, yet He
finds the strength to get up and begin again. His Heart is fixed
on the goal, but His broken body is in agony. Trembling, He
perseveres, ever faithful to His yes.

*Eternal Father, in Your mercy, please help our priests and us to
keep going even when we feel we can't take another step because the
weight of suffering presses upon us. May our yes to follow Christ
be unwavering. For all priests, we ask for the gift of perseverance,
patience, and prayer.*

The Fourth Station: Jesus Meets His Mother
Mother Mary is always there for her Son Jesus, especially in
His darkest hour. Her maternal love strengthens Him each step of
the way. Mother and Son, their two hearts beat in unison always.

*Eternal Father, please help our priests and us to accompany
others in their darkest hour. For all priests, we implore the gifts of
compassion, courage, and patience toward all suffering people.
Please grant that Mary may strengthen priests in their hours of suffering too.*

The Fifth Station: Jesus Is Helped by Simon of Cyrene
Simon is just one of the crowd, a man observing the horror
and mystery unfolding before him. He did not plan to become
part of the drama that day. He is pressed into service. Imagine
the transformation of his heart drawn into such an intimate
encounter with the Suffering Servant.

Suggested Prayers and Offerings for Priests

Eternal Father, strengthen our priests and us to be ready and willing to help anyone who is struggling and in need of assistance. Please heal us of fear or indifference to the poor and grant us the grace of encountering Jesus in His suffering people. For all priests, we pray for the cardinal virtues of prudence, justice, fortitude, and temperance.

The Sixth Station: Veronica Wipes the Face of Jesus

When Jesus is suffering intensely, the attentive Veronica reaches out to the Lord, offering Him an act of kindness. Veronica consoles His aching heart. In the midst of the malicious scene, love prevails.

Eternal Father, please help our priests and us to become vessels of divine mercy. We pray that priests will always be willing to engage in acts of mercy, especially toward people who are faltering on the way. In the midst of malicious rage, love prevails.

The Seventh Station: Jesus Falls the Second Time

Jesus falls again but this time even harder. He gets up again, but it is more difficult because His physical strength is waning. Yet He valiantly carries on. His Sacred Heart is engulfed in the vehemence of divine love. He came to save sinners.

Eternal Father, please bless our priests and us with hope that counteracts discouragement. We all fall and sometimes very often. Repeatedly getting up and starting again is difficult. For all priests, we pray for the grace of hope and joy that strengthens. Grant hearts to be engulfed in the passion of divine love.

The Eighth Station: Jesus Meets the Women of Jerusalem

In the midst of His excruciating pain, Jesus makes the effort to comfort the women who were weeping along the road to Calvary.

They are the only ones with whom He speaks along the Via Dolorosa. He exercises a special esteem for all the women He meets.

Eternal Father, please aid our priests and us not to be so absorbed in personal suffering that we miss the suffering of others in our midst. For all priests, we pray that they will never walk past those who are weeping along the way. Help priests to offer solace and speak words of encouragement whenever needed.

The Ninth Station: Jesus Falls the Third Time

The end of the journey is near, and Jesus falls again. He struggles to get up and continues one last time. The finish line is in sight, but the flesh is so very weak. Yet He will drink the chalice.

Eternal Father, please help our priests and us to pick up our heavy crosses and to persevere when our struggles weigh us down. For all priests, we ask for the grace of complete dependence on Christ's strength, and not on their own. Please grant the clergy increasing trust in divine providence.

The Tenth Station: Jesus Is Stripped of His Garments

Jesus has nothing, not even His clothes—He is stripped of everything in the end. He wills it for love of you and me. Until the end of time, we will gaze upon the One who allowed Himself to be stripped naked.

Eternal Father, Your Son's nakedness covered ours. His Blood became our imperishable garment of salvation. We hurt when we are stripped of anything, but Jesus was stripped of everything. For all priests, we beg for the grace of spiritual poverty, simplicity, purity, and hearts willing to be vulnerable.

The Eleventh Station: Jesus Is Nailed to the Cross

The pain intensifies with each blow of the hammer on the nail that pierces His sacred hands and feet. Each blow is a vivid reminder of the sin of the world that weighs upon Him. He takes it upon Himself because He loves. This is the fire He longed to kindle.

Eternal Father, You so loved the world that You sent Your Son Jesus to save us. How can we possibly thank You for such an ineffable Gift? Graciously help our priests to be lifted up with Jesus on the wooden bed of divine love with arms outstretched to embrace the whole Church with mercy.

The Twelfth Station: Jesus Dies on the Cross

It is finished. Jesus suffered inestimable, complete torment on the Cross. He surrendered all: "Father, into thy hands I commit my spirit!" (Luke 23:46). Yet He extended mercy, full pardon, and forgiveness to those who condemned and crucified Him. He even promised Paradise to the "good thief" before He breathed His last.

Eternal Father, graciously grant our priests and us the grace to forgive as Christ forgives. For all priests, we implore the grace of surrender to the divine. Help them to echo the words of Jesus: "Father, into Thy hands . . ." Guide priests to place everything into Your hands and hang on to Jesus only.

The Thirteenth Station: Jesus Is Taken Down from the Cross

The Lord's lifeless, battered body is laid in His Mother's arms. Imagine the perfect sorrow of Mary as she embraces and kisses her Son, bone of her bone and flesh of her flesh. The sword of Simeon's prophecy has thoroughly pierced her Immaculate Heart. Does she despair? No! Yet, what perfect maternal sorrow and faith!

Eternal Father, please bless our priests and us with a new awareness of the inestimable value of Marian devotion and consecration. For all priests, we implore that they take Mary as their spiritual mother and consecrate their priesthood to her. May all priests be held in Mary's protective, maternal love.

The Fourteenth Station: Jesus Is Laid in the Tomb

Then the earth quakes. Silence ensues, and darkness engulfs. For Jesus, the tomb is a place of transition — a place between death and new life. He is doing a new thing since nothing would ever be the same again.

Eternal Father, sometimes we feel lost and afraid when we are in a place between darkness and light, between death and new life. Shake us up and out of our self-made tombs so that we can become a new creation in Christ. For all priests, we implore the gift of sanctifying transformation.[119]

⚜

The Foundation of Prayer for Priests invites you to become a member of the global family of intercessors for priests and seminarians by visiting the website www.foundationforpriests.org.

---

[119] The Stations of the Cross for Priests and Laity are available as a printable trifold at www.foundationforpriests.org.

~

About the Author

Kathleen Beckman, L.H.S., wife, mother, and business owner, is the President and Co-founder of the Foundation of Prayer for Priests (www.foundationforpriests.org), an international apostolate of prayer and catechesis for the holiness of priests. Kathleen has served the Church for twenty-five years as a Catholic evangelist, author, Ignatian certified retreat director, radio host, and writer. In her diocese she serves as the lay coordinator of exorcism and deliverance ministry, having completed courses on liberation from evil at Mundelein Seminary and in Rome. She sits on the advisory board of Magnificat, A Ministry to Catholic Women, and the Pope Leo XIII Institute. Often featured on Catholic media — EWTN Radio and TV, Radio Maria, and the Catholic Channel — she enthusiastically proclaims the joy of the gospel.

Sophia Institute

Sophia Institute is a nonprofit institution that seeks to nurture the spiritual, moral, and cultural life of souls and to spread the Gospel of Christ in conformity with the authentic teachings of the Roman Catholic Church.

Sophia Institute Press fulfills this mission by offering translations, reprints, and new publications that afford readers a rich source of the enduring wisdom of mankind.

Sophia Institute also operates the popular online resource CatholicExchange.com. *Catholic Exchange* provides world news from a Catholic perspective as well as daily devotionals and articles that will help readers to grow in holiness and live a life consistent with the teachings of the Church.

In 2013, Sophia Institute launched Sophia Institute for Teachers to renew and rebuild Catholic culture through service to Catholic education. With the goal of nurturing the spiritual, moral, and cultural life of souls, and an abiding respect for the role and work of teachers, we strive to provide materials and programs that are at once enlightening to the mind and ennobling to the heart; faithful and complete, as well as useful and practical.

Sophia Institute gratefully recognizes the Solidarity Association for preserving and encouraging the growth of our apostolate over the course of many years. Without their generous and timely support, this book would not be in your hands.

www.SophiaInstitute.com
www.CatholicExchange.com
www.SophiaInstituteforTeachers.org

Sophia Institute Press® is a registered trademark of Sophia Institute.
Sophia Institute is a tax-exempt institution as defined by the
Internal Revenue Code, Section 501(c)(3). Tax I.D. 22-2548708.